Dedication

To my husband, Tom, because I believe you are the most devoted, faithful, understanding, and patient man I know. God truly blessed me when he led you to a broken girl and caused your love for her to be an example of His—unconditional, unchanging, and everlasting. Thank you for being an Ephesians 5:25 husband and a man after God's own heart. You certainly have mine, for I love you and it's with gratitude and deep affection that I dedicate this book to you.

Warning:

This book contains graphic sexual material and is not suitable for a younger reading audience. Reader discretion advised.

Dear Eric
Psalm 34:5 says
it well, "They look to
Him and are radiant;
their faces never blush
with shame
or confusion." AMP

But I *Liked* It...
and Other Lies

*Overcoming the Shame
of Sexual Abuse*

Roxanne Fawley

I think there's
a powerful story in
you, also! if you ever need
help with it or a beta
Reader... rocksand5@gmail.com

5 Fold Media
Visit us at www.5foldmedia.com

Contents

Foreword

To me, God is patient. As we are being perfected into the image of His Son Jesus Christ, we must let His patience mold us (James 1:4 NKJV). I have seen Christians become tired of the journey toward perfection and give up trying to grow. Others don't even begin to allow the Holy Spirit to work in them; they see salvation as the end of the adventure rather than the beginning. When I met her, Roxanne had certainly taken the first step toward humility. She saw her lack of worth apart from God—except she wasn't apart from God anymore. However, she clung to the delusion that her life experiences had made her too worthless for God's grace. "Surely God is good to others, but in my case...."

Roxanne has been a real encouragement to me. I have seen her perseverance despite her self-contempt. She realized that there was nowhere else to go, so she clung to the Lord and His Word. I was thrilled as I watched the Lord work in her, drawing her from prideful self-contempt into humble acknowledgement that:

True: in me dwells no good thing, all my righteousness is filthy rags.

But also true: Christ is in me, so I can do and am doing all things; I have infinite value and infinite security; I am perfectly clean.

She has found balance to add to her patient perseverance as she rests in God's infinite grace. So can you as you relate to her story. Just remember, it is a journey. So be patient—God is not finished with you. Paul says, "Not that I have already attained, or am already perfected; but I press on, that I may lay hold of that for which Christ Jesus has also laid hold of me" (Philippians 3:12 NKJV).

God will show you that no sin, no defilement, no pit can do anything other than serve as a measure of His grace. How big is grace? Grace that is greater than all Roxanne's sin, all your sin, and all my sin as well.

> - Verle L. Bell, M.D. Slave of Christ, husband of Lois, father of five, and doting grandfather of, so far, seven.

Prologue

Who comforts (consoles and encourages) us in every trouble (calamity and affliction), so that we may also be able to comfort (console and encourage) those who are in any kind of trouble or distress, with the comfort (consolation and encouragement) with which we ourselves are comforted (consoled or encouraged) by God (2 Corinthians 1:4).

A low murmur of conversation filled the white tents, punctuated intermittently with laughter. As I made my way past tables toward the house, I was stopped here and there by people who were leaving. "We're taking off now, Roxanne, congratulations again! We'll go find Tom before we go. Great party, thanks for having us! Just imagine, forty years! That's really something to celebrate these days!"

As I opened the sliding doors and stepped into the house, I heard a rumble of thunder in the distance, and silently thanked the Lord again that the kids had rented the tents. It had rained on and off again all day. The rain itself was a blessing in disguise, because it had been unbearably hot and humid for the past several days. Now, at least the temperature had fallen a bit and there was a breeze, making the tent area much more comfortable. There was no way we would have been able to fit sixty people in the house!

But I Liked It...and Other Lies

Sixty people, forty years—our children were throwing us an anniversary party! I still had to pinch myself. I took a moment to look around and marveled quietly again.

A few short years ago, I wondered if my children would even want a relationship with me when they became adults. Now, I was gazing at the results of weeks of work and expense on *their* part to make Tom and me happy today. Casey, 36; Suzy, 34; Jaynie, 29; and Mia, 21, had all worked together to give us a day of unforgettable memories.

Our creative daughters had set up a large board with old pictures of us in the shape of a huge number 40. On the same table, they had placed a basket of cards and pens so our guests could share their memories of us or wish us well. Unbeknownst to us, they had also requested the guests give us gift certificates to nearby restaurants as our presents. Tom and I now had enough for date-night dinners for the whole year!

Our huge cake had been designed to match the invitations and it was beautiful. The invitations were grass green with a white birch tree off to one side. Carved on the tree trunk were our initials inside a heart. The girls and Casey had arranged for all the food, and it was a delicious menu. Even Kyle, Mia's fiancé, had shown what a great cook he was with the pulled pork and coleslaw he contributed.

I smiled down at our three grandchildren, playing on the living room floor. What a blessed life I have, I thought, and how few people know about the long battle that raged on behind the scenes.

There had been forty years of marriage, but only the last six of them had been deeply happy. How I used to long and pray for Tom to have a loving wife who desired him. The kind of woman he deserved to have. Only an all-powerful, gracious

Roxanne Fawley

God could make me into that woman. I am a loving wife now. I love Tom completely—with my words, actions, and thoughts. Only God knew all along that this day was coming.

For most of my life I had a dark, depressing secret. I believed the lie I had liked the sexual abuse I had experienced as a youth, that the incestuous relationship I had with my father was consensual. The guilt and shame of that lie! It took years before I found the courage to say the words out loud to anyone. I believed I was alone in this because, of course, sexual abuse was hated by every other victim. I kept the secret to myself; I would have preferred to die rather than admit I had such evil traits.

Secrets are powerful and dangerous, especially when they are lies.

Why tell my story now? Because if I had read of a case like mine, where the victim thought she enjoyed and even sought abuse, I might have had the courage to tell my counselors I held the same belief. I might have been spared years of self-torture caused by the lies; instead I considered myself unusual, evil, and undeserving of any help. I felt exempt from every offer of comfort because I never believed I was a true victim. After all, I had sometimes been so willing. I had always received pleasure, not pain, from the hand of my sexual abuser. Because of beliefs like these, I concluded I was wicked, with a sick and twisted character.

The truth can be found in an excellent definition of this kind of abuse by Dr. Dan Allender: "Sexual abuse is any contact or interaction (visual, verbal, or psychological) between a child/adolescent and an adult when the child/adolescent is being used for the sexual stimulation of the perpetrator or any other person." That is who my father was and what he did.

11

But I Liked It...and Other Lies

Not until the age of fifty-four, after attending intense therapy, did I finally confess my secret and learn the truth. I had been a true victim. All the years of believing I was responsible for my abuse were just as harmful to my psyche as if I'd believed I was completely helpless.

"But I liked it"…and other lies were what prevented me from being spiritually, emotionally, and physically healthy. Lies and condemning thoughts pervaded my soul, like: *I'm to blame. I enjoyed it. I was old enough to know better. I asked for it.* Or, *He was drunk, so I was the responsible one.*

Was I really? Did I really? It is my prayer that my story will be used to set others free from such torturous lies.

Chapter 1: Once Upon a Time...

But Jesus called them [the parents] to Him, saying,
Allow the little children to come to Me, and do not
hinder them, for to such [as these] belongs the
kingdom of God (Luke 18:16).

There was a time when neighborhood kids played *outside* more than *in*, weather permitting—and sometimes even if it didn't. A simple time when doors were rarely locked and neighborhood watch signs were unnecessary. That's just what neighbors routinely did for each other. This is how it was in my early years. We would often gather at the schoolyard located at the end of our street for impromptu games of softball or football, depending on the season. No matter what one's gender or age, everyone was welcomed. (My favorite times were when my mom would join us in the fun.) We could, and often did, stay at our playing until we could no longer make out the ball in the fading light, or until we were summoned by our mothers. It was an idyllic time; we felt safe and carefree outside. What a contrast to the dark and uncertain atmosphere churning inside my home.

I was raised in the small, pleasant, middle-class community of Oakwood in Kalamazoo, Michigan. The streets were tree-lined, with rows of bungalows and two-story houses built before World War II steadfastly facing each other through an array of hedges and picket fences. Some sections of sidewalk were cracked and misshapen from the pressure of overgrown, gnarly roots from the old oak, maple, and walnut trees. Their long, intertwined branches reached across the streets to each other, creating a canopy that seemed to shelter us from the outside world. However, it wasn't the world outside we were threatened by.

Like most kids, we always looked forward to summers with impatient anticipation. Our neighborhood bordered Woods Lake where we had our own community beach, complete with a dock and a high dive. There was also a concession stand where we spent our twenty-five cent allowances on packages of candy or chips and pop. The beach was owned by the neighborhood association. We held car washes, ice cream socials and dances, along with beach parties complete with food and music to raise the funds for employing a lifeguard. This also maintained the beach and kept the concession stand well stocked. There were beach cleanup days, where we all pitched in and helped pick up litter. One day each season, we would rake the sand of its slimy weeds and other debris that had washed up on shore over the winter. Each summer every family who wanted to enjoy the beach had to pay a five-dollar membership fee for the privilege. We were provided with little patches that our mothers sewed onto our swimsuits which allowed us to enter through the chain-link gate, towel in hand, slick with sunblock. We alternated on hot summer days from frolicking in the cool water to basking in the sun on our beach towels spread over the warm sand. Moreover, through the woods to the right of the beach, about one quarter of the way around the lake, the city of Kalamazoo also maintained a beach, a tad larger, but with much the same amenities. Sometimes we would trek through the woods to the city side to check it out; but in the end, we smugly returned to the Oakwood side, our own private haven, not to be shared with outsiders.

In those days, summers seemed to last forever. We took the lovely sunshine for granted as we idled away our carefree days, doing whatever we pleased. We were always on the alert for the tinkling bells of the ice cream man as he peddled through the streets with his never-ending supply of popsicles, ice cream cones covered with chocolate and nuts, and an assortment of our favorite ice cream bars. We were fascinated when he would open the top of his portable freezer and tufts of cold air escaped from blocks of dry ice and mixed with the summer heat, only to immediately disappear before our eyes. Proud of ourselves for saving our allowances, we couldn't wait for our chosen treats to be brought up from the frosty depths. We'd cautiously stand back so as not to get too close and possibly get burned by the seemingly magical ice.

On days when it rained, we went to the neighbor's to play board games with bowls of chips and bottles of pop close at hand. We never invited other kids to our house. Sometimes we took our time, splashing in puddles, squishing soft mud through our bare toes, enjoying the fresh ambiance that comes after a summer rain shower and appreciating air cleansed of dust and pollen. The world felt fresh.

Even though I was living in a grossly dysfunctional environment, I didn't know at the time just how off kilter we were. The four of us played and squabbled like all brothers and sisters do. We looked forward to Halloween, Christmas, and our weekly visits to our maternal grandparents' house. They lived on Reynolds Lake, a glorious body of water in Lawrence, Michigan, a town about thirty miles away.

But I Liked It...and Other Lies

We rode bikes, played games, and did chores. Our mother, like most moms, stayed home and had dinner on the table every night at six o'clock.

Everything changed the summer I turned twelve. My entire view of the world shifted, resulting in an almost tangible shattering of my innocence. My childhood ended with a splintering of my soul that hurled the damaged fragments every which way, embedding jagged shards deep in my mind. Some immediately caused such pain that I didn't think I deserved to live. Others remained buried so deep they were forgotten for a while, until they worked themselves to the surface over the next forty years to wreak such havoc within me that I thought I was evil personified. Before my twelfth birthday, my father set in motion events that would lead us both down paths to hell on earth. His choices ultimately led to his demise at the age of forty-five. However, through the grace of God and the unwavering support of my amazing husband, I was finally able to abandon such a horrific course. This is my journey.

Chapter 2: There's Always a Villain

A man of wrath stirs up strife, and a man given to anger commits and causes much transgression (Proverbs 29:22).

My father, George, was a disturbed man. He was as handsome and brilliant as he was violent and bad tempered. However, as is often the case with troubled people, he could hide it well. He ruled our home with calculated cruelty and truly sociopathic behavior. I believe, for reasons deeply ingrained in him from his own troubled childhood, evil did lurk. It was an ugly part of his personality, released from whatever weak self-restraint he may have been able to exercise by his daily consumption of alcohol, until eventually even sober, he was mean to the point of cruelty and evil to the point of perversion.

My father, the second son of four boys, was born on April 30, 1926, to my grandparents, Michael and Frances Moran. Grandpa was born in Ireland and was the stereotypical drunken Irishman. Of his four sons, only my father inherited the disease. My grandma was his second wife. I learned well into my teens that grandpa's first wife had taken their small daughter and left him. No one in my family ever met this half-sister.

Grandma converted to Catholicism in order to marry grandpa. (I think there was something about a papal annulment regarding the first marriage.) Grandma took her new religion and her marriage vows very seriously. She became a dutiful wife and eventually an enabler, loving her boys and trying to protect them, all the while excusing their father. My father witnessed firsthand a man's cruelty toward his family and vowed he'd "never be like him." I ache for the small, innocent child he was, and have finally learned not to separate the father I knew from the boy he once was, as I have come to forgive him through the grace of God.

My father was passionately proud of his Irish heritage, preferring to be called "Irish" instead of George. After his stint in the Navy when he served on a ship in the South Pacific, he took advantage of the GI Bill to attend a local university and graduated with a degree in teaching. He eventually got a job in the nearby school system, teaching history and English to junior high students. This is where he remained until his death in 1972.

Somehow he was able to maintain an aura of respect within the teaching community. This was partly due to his cunning ability to charm and fool most people, and partly due to the fact that for some reason, known only to those involved, he was shielded and protected by his peers whenever his "illness" spilled over into his daytime life. Every now and then rumors would surface, hinting at his drinking on the job or his having bottles of alcohol hidden in his desk, but nothing ever came of them. In spite of everything, he was an excellent teacher. He was known for his disciplinarian skills and charisma, and parents loved him—even if the kids didn't.

In the early years of his career, my father would make a little extra money coaching basketball or archery after school. During the summers, he would work at one of the local creameries or in the sports department at a local store. However, as his disease progressed, most summers meant

18

he was home all day, sitting in his chair—usually wearing only boxer shorts. He'd idly drink his favorite beer, with the ever-present wispy thread of smoke wafting up from the end of his cigarette, and making all our lives miserable. George Moran lived two lives. One as a respected, well-dressed professional—he owned five suits with five matching bow ties. I always knew what day of the week it was by the color of his suit. The other was a slovenly, feared alcoholic. My earliest memories of him are shrouded with fear. So much fighting! So much turmoil!

My mother, Maxine, was a beautiful, brown-haired, brown-eyed naïve girl when she met my father. She entered this world on January 17, 1928, the last of five children born in the first six years of her parents, Paul and Florence Jungel's, marriage. Ever trusting, she got pregnant the night she became engaged. Filled with trepidation, but with the approval of her parents, on November 22, 1948 my parents married in a small, intimate ceremony. The abuse began soon after.

My father revealed a cruel streak he had been able to keep carefully hidden throughout the twenty-one months of their courtship. My parents saw each other only on Saturdays and one day during the week, making it easy for him to role-play the charming beau. She never suspected a thing. The abuse began verbally. He would accuse my mother of all kinds of preposterous wrongdoing, such as infidelity and lying. He would say terrible, hurtful things and even wondered out loud if the baby was his. He never really believed any of this was true, but in his drunken paranoia, he lashed out with the sole intent to hurt. I have often thought that deep down my father knew he wasn't good enough for my mother. He'd attack in fear, as a bully often does, to squelch the spirit of his victim, just to keep the upper hand. My mother, with all of her

19

inexperience and the limited resources available in the 1940s, resigned herself to her new, turbulent life.

It wasn't long before the abuse turned violent. It began with a shove and eventually escalated to the point that he actually caused her to fall down their apartment stairs. It mattered little to him that she was expecting their first child. She was never hurt enough to seek medical attention; but over the years, I witnessed black eyes, cuts, bruises—and once, he even knocked out her existing bottom teeth and broke her upper dentures. When he was sober he was always sorry, vowing to never let it happen again. But of course it did... again and again and again.

Adding to her distress was the shame she felt. She managed to hide the abuse well from those outside, even her family. The only people with whom she ever dared share this degrading part of her life were the local police. (They could do nothing but offer to have her file a complaint on Monday.) Oh, and then there was our parish priest, who counseled her with the admonishment that divorce was out of the question. She needed to forgive him and try not to provoke him.

Soon after their marriage, my mother was dismayed to learn that her husband possessed a voracious sexual appetite. He would often want her three or more times a day. She had no way to know this was not normal. No one spoke of such things. Moreover, she hated being with him when he was drunk, which was soon becoming an everyday occurrence. The battles were endless.

After she had my brother, Marty James, the criticisms and abuse extended to include her mothering. The baby was dark complexioned like my mother and had her brown eyes instead of my dad's blue ones. My father continued the inference that

20

Marty couldn't be his. He was a remarkable baby though, who could stand at three months and was walking at seven months. Since my mother had not had the opportunity to be around babies that much, she took it in stride.

My father saw competition for my mother's affection in his son and soon began to voice his disapproval of her parenting skills. He'd chide that she coddled the boy too much when as an infant she rocked him in her arms to comfort him. He'd say she was making a sissy out of him if she hugged him too much as a toddler. As a small boy, Marty was not allowed to sit close to her on the sofa. Before he entered kindergarten, my brother was given chores way beyond his years, such as painting the fence and fixing the porch steps. He was often the target of my father's sadistic sense of humor and his swift hand. My mother dared not intervene when this happened. Experience had taught her it would go much easier on Marty and her if she kept quiet.

When Marty was two and a half years old, my sister, Kathy Ann, was born. She was a beautiful, shy baby girl who possessed the "required" blue eyes. It wasn't long before Marty assumed the role of "big brother," a role he continued to play until he was drafted into the army at nineteen. Kathy spent her earliest years tagging along after Marty whenever she could. Following his lead and obeying his commands, she was his own personal toady to command, no matter how mischievous the deed. He was her hero, and amid all the turmoil she had known since birth, she felt safe in his presence.

When my mother found herself pregnant again when Kathy was only nine months old, she was not too thrilled. So much so that she did not seek prenatal care until she was seven months along. She had taken one of the kids in to see the doctor and he remarked that he expected her to come see

21

him too...soon. My father's shirts couldn't quite conceal what she had been trying to hide for months. She has since told me that it wasn't that she didn't *want* me, she just didn't feel it was the right time, so soon after Kathy. Things were not any better between her and my father. His outbursts and rages were unpredictable and his target was usually the closest person in his proximity. She was mentally and physically exhausted. Between the stress of constantly being on high alert for her husband's mood swings and caring for two small children with another on the way, my mother was enduring it all the best way she knew how—silently stoic and all alone.

On August 12, 1953, I was born into this volatile family. My mother named me Roxanne after a model on an old game show she used to watch. I guess she thought Roxanne was a long enough name because I didn't get a middle name, just Roxanne. Back in the early fifties, one had to be baptized with a saint's name. Since there weren't any Saint Roxannes that she knew of, I was baptized Ann. (My sister was also baptized Ann because her legal name was Kathy, not the more formal Kathleen or Katherine. The church is much more lenient now and parents can name and baptize their children almost anything they want.) Even though I was a surprise, my mother always told me I was a blessing. She has said I was the easiest baby to have and care for, and she would have liked to have had a dozen more if they could've all been like me. Of course she exaggerates, but it makes me smile.

As a small child I was friendly and trusting; I never met a stranger and feared no one. Not the sort of traits that would tend to keep a child safe. Kathy, on the other hand, always seemed wary. She shied away from strangers and rarely spoke outside of the family. In hindsight, it's not surprising I became the object of my father's sick obsession.

Roxanne Fawley

The youngest child to be born of this unstable union was my brother, Kevin Patrick, on April 30, 1957, my father's thirty-first birthday. I was four years old and remember that Kathy and I had to stay with my uncle and aunt for two extra weeks before we could go home to meet the baby. We had been exposed to measles at our cousins. Our stay was supposed to have been only for a few days, but they could not take a chance and expose the baby.

My uncle was my father's brother, and while not a heavy drinker he did possess a strict disciplinary attitude and never spared the rod—for even the smallest of wrongdoings. But this was "normal" in my world. I remember having to sleep in a crib and having a nightmare resulting in my wetting the bed, which ended with me getting spanked.

From the very beginning, Kevin was the darling of the family. He was cute and had the bluest eyes ever. He was chubby cheeked and giggly, and we all adored him. My father was especially proud of him, and indeed Kevin did resemble him the most. However, it didn't protect him from the fear and pain we all experienced at our father's whims. Marty's role as protector continued, but we all felt it our duty to shield Kevin from the vicious evil lurking in the shadows, ever ready to lash out without warning. Kevin was fourteen when our father died. We all think he was the lucky one.

It's a fact that our entire childhood was encased in dread. My siblings and I never knew from day to day, or even moment to moment, what to expect from our father. We developed a sixth sense of being able to walk into a room and instinctively read the atmosphere. Unfortunately, my father's moods could change quickly from just plain mean and indifferent to explosively violent. We often couldn't avoid the all too common swift slaps or the "go get the belt and wait

23

for me" beatings. He was sadistic about the latter, and would order whichever of us was his victim at the time to go into his bedroom, undress from the waist down, and lie across the bed. Then we would have to wait and wait in total submission until he decided to come in and close the door. I'm sure he derived a sick pleasure from this entire process—from savoring the anticipated thrashing to the satisfaction of his ability to subject us to terror and suffering without intervention. *He* had the power; *he* had all the control. Sometimes he would carry out these "punishments" when our mother was not at home, but frequently she would be in the next room, silent and helpless. She knew if she tried to interfere it would be much worse for her and us.

When my mother was his intended target, he would order us kids up the steep narrow stairway to the converted attic where we slept. Once the door was closed, however, we would quietly scoot back down. We would cluster together on the bottom step, barely breathing lest he hear us, and listen for the dreaded sound of fist hitting flesh. All the while, a constant torrent of profanity, accusations, and threats spewed from his mouth. These caused injuries without leaving marks, every bit as harmful as his blows. Trembling with anxiety, we were fearful that he might fatally hurt her.

Once while we were huddled together, I remember Marty fervently whispering, "I want to punch him and kick him!" He vowed to Kathy and me he was going to save us and Mom too. His passion and anger were far more evident than his fear. Marty was only eight years old, and unbeknownst to us at the time, his words proved to be prophetic.

Chapter 3: So It Began

But whoever causes one of these little ones who believe in and acknowledge and cleave to Me to stumble and sin [that is, who entices him or hinders him in right conduct or thought], it would be better (more expedient and profitable or advantageous) for him to have a great millstone fastened around his neck and to be sunk in the depth of the sea (Matthew 18:6).

U p until I was eleven years old, the only physical contact I'd ever received from my father was painful. I had never known the kind of warm hugs, gentle admonishments, or playful banter my friends seemed to share with their fathers. He was nothing like the fathers on TV or in the books I read. The father-daughter relationship I so longed for eluded me, leaving a void deep within I never expected to have filled. I now know that my father had been shrewdly preparing me to be his victim for my entire childhood.

That summer we had an old septic tank removed from our back yard. Oakwood had recently been annexed by the city of Kalamazoo; therefore each household was forced to comply with all city ordinances and hook up to the city sewer. Our neighbors were forced to get rid of their outhouse and put in an indoor bathroom! As a result, there remained a huge hole in our yard, just outside our back door. One day, before my parents were able to have the gap filled in, we were outside playing with some neighbor kids. Due to one mischievous boy,

But I Liked It...and Other Lies

I ended up falling into that rancid hole. I was not physically hurt but shortly afterward became gravely ill. At first the doctors suspected mononucleosis because I was utterly exhausted all the time. Then they thought I might have appendicitis due to my nausea and vomiting. This was also ruled out, and I continued to worsen. When my skin turned yellow, they finally came up with the correct diagnosis—hepatitis B. This was a serious matter. The whole neighborhood had at one time or another been in contact with me, not to mention the hospital ward to which I had been briefly admitted (when they thought I had appendicitis). They all had to get gamma globulin shots. How had I contracted it in the first place? The conclusion was: I had been exposed to the nasty germs during my encounter with the septic pit.

I was in the hospital for two weeks, and the doctor actually told my mother I might die. There was a prayer circle started for me by the ladies in our church. Prayer is powerful, and even though complete recovery didn't happen overnight, I did disprove the doctors' predictions. I fully recovered before the start of a new school year, which in itself was a true miracle. A damaged liver and a lifelong ban on ever being a blood donor were direct results of this unfortunate tumble. It was also the beginning of the waking nightmare soon to become my life.

After my discharge from the hospital, the doctors ordered lots of rest as a precaution against a possible relapse. One Sunday morning I felt too weak to get up and go to Mass with my mother and siblings. (By this time, my father hadn't attended church with us in years.) He and I were alone in the house. The only bathroom in our house was downstairs. Needing to use it, I quietly came down from the bedroom I shared with my sister. I slipped past my father who was passed out in his chair, still drunk from the night before. When I came out, however, he was awake. He called me over to his chair and asked me to lift up my nightgown so he could check my stomach and chest for a rash. He said the German measles were going around his school and he would be able to tell if I had them by looking. I did as he asked. I knew I was not supposed to get sick with even the slightest cold because my immune system had been compromised by the hepatitis. His reasoning seemed sound and his caring, oddly genuine. Embarrassment at having my father see my underpants was overshadowed by this new feeling of—*what, love?* From Dad? He then proceeded to touch me gently as he examined me. This new kind of contact from my father confused me.

All the weeks I was in the hospital, he never once came up to see me. Years earlier, when Kathy was five years old, she spent a month in the hospital in traction after having broken her leg. He never visited her either. As she had with Kathy, my mother came up to see me twice a day, every day. It was delightful having her all to myself, and I was delighted with all her attention. She ran a small day care out of our home in order to supplement my father's income, and to help compensate for the money he drank away. I was fully aware how difficult it was for her to make the ten-mile round trip twice a day. Given our family's history, I did not miss having my father visit at all.

The truth was, I loved being in the hospital. Everyone was so nice and caring. My meals were brought to me on a tray and I didn't have any chores. I could sleep as much as I wanted, or read all day long if I preferred. I also received get-well cards every day. I was so happy there that I began to cry when the doctor said I was well enough to go home. He assumed my tears were those of joy. The truth? I was distressed by the thought of going back to the war zone my home had become.

But I Liked It...and Other Lies

After my father's alleged search for a rash, he asked me to get an illustrated Bible storybook and read out loud to him, since neither of us had gone to church and it was Sunday, after all. He had me sit on his lap. I can still feel the rise and fall of his chest from his breathing and his warm breath on my arm. Every exhale was stale with a mixture of cigarettes and beer. He reeked of a popular cologne as if he bathed in it, which I now think he did in the hopes he could mask the smell of alcohol. To this day, I can pick out the man in a crowd that prefers this particular scent, and it turns my stomach.

I began to read the story of Noah's ark, which had always held a grim fascination for me. I remember every detail of the illustration depicting the great flood. The image artfully drawn was nevertheless horrible to behold. People were clinging to trees and climbing mountains in an effort to flee the rising water. One especially troubling scene was of a mother's single arm rising up through the water, desperately holding her infant above the surface in a futile attempt to save its life. I was so sad when I thought of all the babies that drowned. It was too much for my young mind to grasp. I wondered for years at the seemingly harsh punishment of innocent children just because their parents did not believe in Noah's God. I was glad that I believed, though, and wondered if my dad did. Even though I doubted it, I was not about to ask him, for fear of making him angry. Experience had taught me his moods could turn quickly without much notice, and he was being uncharacteristically kind; I didn't want to break the spell. He even paid me a compliment; he told me I was reading well. I couldn't recall his ever saying anything encouraging to me before. Usually, when he noticed me at all it would be to cruelly criticize or taunt me about my lisp or some other flaw, real or imagined.

That was all there was to it that day, but a seed had been planted. It soon took root and sprouted into a sprig of curiosity. *Did my father actually like me? Could he be a daddy like other kids had?* The craving deep within my heart nourished the little sprig of curiosity into a real need to know. I wanted to again feel the gentle touch he surprised me with the first time. A few weeks later I stayed home from Mass again. This time *I* asked *him* to check me for measles. I was so easy.

So it began. He proceeded to tenderly check me all over. Although I was a little embarrassed, I did love it. When he was finished with the examination, he told me a new kind of story, one about when he was in the Navy. He was given a young prostitute for his use. She was only my age, so he said he couldn't be with her, "in that way." He felt she was too young, he told me virtuously, but he did give her a good feeling. I was sitting on his footstool in front of him when he said it. Ever so lightly, he touched me between my legs with his toe. It felt good to me too. He said he could give *me* a good feeling if I wanted. I did.

He took me up on his lap and began to touch me. At the tender age of eleven my father prematurely awakened me sexually. It had felt so good. All the new sensations and thoughts coursed through my body and mind in a jumble of confusion. In just a few seconds he had stolen my childhood and shattered my innocence forever. All I knew was it felt wonderful. I loved it. I had no idea of the horrific harm it had done, or how it would plague me for the greater part of my life.

When it was over, I pushed his hand away. I felt in control. He said I was a good girl for knowing when to stop. I was confused even more by what just happened when he called me his "precious Roxannie" and told me not to tell anyone about us because they wouldn't understand. He said he loved and needed me because my mother didn't love him anymore. I knew it was true that she didn't love him. I also knew why. He was brutal toward her. I did feel special, but did I love him? He was so different to me now. Nice and attentive. I was just a little afraid that my family would guess the reason why. I knew in my heart that what we were doing was wrong if it had to be hidden. It was easy to keep it a secret though. I didn't want anyone to know either.

Prior to all of this, I had been the one he'd singled out most often for his special brand of cruelty. When I was a baby, he was afraid I was tongue-tied. One night, in a drunken stupor, he decided to correct this perceived flaw. He took scissors and clumsily snipped my lingual frenulum (the cord that stretches from underneath the tongue to the floor of the mouth). It resulted in my having a speech impediment. Far from being tongue-tied, my tongue was now too loose. It made it difficult for me to enunciate words, especially "S" words like soldier and shoulder. I remember having to learn to say, "She sells sea shells by the seashore," over and over. I would get mocked or spanked if I said it wrong. To this day, I sometimes struggle with these words, especially when I talk a great deal or I'm tired.

I also sucked my thumb, which was unacceptable to him. I had to wear a sock on my hand when he was around. Due to a tonsil and adenoid problem, I was a mouth-breather, which infuriated him. He said I looked stupid with my mouth hanging open and he taped my mouth shut. I wouldn't be able to breathe except through a tiny crack in the tape. I had nightmares of suffocating for the longest time, even into adulthood.

Being treated special was wonderful and scary at the same time. Sitting by him used to be my punishment. Now I began to look for times I could be alone with him. Saturdays were the only days my mother could do her errands or go shopping. Because on weekends he would be well into his beer by late morning, the other kids would make themselves scarce once Mom left. I had only to stand by his chair, and he'd say, "All righty," then on his lap I'd go. You know the rest.

My father was never sober when he touched me. From the time he got home from work around 4:30 p.m. until he passed out in his chair, there would be an open bottle of beer on his end table. In the kitchen, a nightly bag of empties would pile up. I'd sneak downstairs when everyone was asleep and go to him. Over time things got progressively worse. He began to show me pornography. (To this day I can see every lewd picture he showed me like it was burned into my brain. If only God's Word were so easily retained.) I was getting older and he was getting bolder. He wanted more from me. He would have me touch his genitals and tell me I was the reason he would get hard. He would get excited by the emergence of my maturing body.

The second to the last time I was with my father in a sexual way was a lovely Saturday afternoon. A gentle breeze came in from the open window. I could hear the simple, everyday sounds of the neighborhood—kids playing in the schoolyard, a dog barking, and the drone of a lawn mower. The sounds I had always taken comfort in hearing without even thinking about it. I became keenly aware of the paradox I was living and felt eerily disconnected. Everything around me was normal, while I felt like everything in me was off balance and unreal.

He told me to take off all my clothes and get into his bed. He was completely naked. For the first time he was very demanding, and for the first time, I hesitated. He became insistent, and a spark of the old fear instantly ignited within

31

me. Afraid that someone could come home at any time, I nevertheless complied.

He kissed me on the mouth and forced his tongue between my clenched lips. I hated it! He said he wouldn't put himself in me, but I knew in my gut the unspoken word in his statement was "yet." It *was* going to lead to it this time. Then he put his face between my legs and brought me to climax. It all happened so fast. My mind was reeling when I pushed his head away. Simultaneously feeling selfish and guilty, I grabbed my clothes and ran out of the room. When I looked back, he was just lying there, holding his genitals and saying, "What about me?" I was repulsed, but knew then for certain that he had been planning on having intercourse with me. I was now fourteen years old and only too aware that I could become pregnant. It had to stop!

I sought refuge in the bathroom, trying unsuccessfully to calm my breathing and compose myself. My mind was whirling with muddled thoughts. *How did I become a part of this? I am the most evil person in the whole world. I hate myself! No one can ever, ever know.*

Being older, I could no longer find any kind of justification for what I'd done. In truth, I had not felt innocent for quite some time. I stood staring at my reflection in the mirror for so long I imagined my face morphing into that of a monster. Frozen with revulsion, I couldn't move, or even look away. I could only think about what had just happened, and what had almost happened. I was filled with dread at the possibility of what might happen if there was a next time. As the human mind will often do in horrendous situations to protect sanity, everything, even the mirror disappeared. My brain shut down; it had reached its limit. I can't remember how long I was in the bathroom. I do remember though, when I came to myself, my father was sitting in his chair, beer in hand, smoke rising from the cigarette in his ashtray as if nothing had happened. For a split second, my fragile mind wondered if perhaps it hadn't.

At the end of the rutted alley that ran behind the garages on our street lived Lois. She was my best friend then, and is still one of my best friends today, I'm very thankful to say. She was a beautiful, sweet-natured teenager, with blue eyes and thick brown hair. She was always a joy to be around. (She is the same way today.) Although she was two years older than me and only one year older than my sister, we got along the best. Sometimes the three of us hung out together, but at fifteen, Kathy hadn't outgrown her shyness, and felt awkward in most social situations.

It was often to Lois' house I would escape, and this day was no different. Considering what I had just been through, I was surprised when Lois welcomed me as if nothing had happened. My shame felt tangible, as if it must be visible to the naked eye. I didn't feel normal; how could I possibly look normal?

I became like a robot programmed to act human. *Smile, talk, laugh*, I commanded myself, all the while convinced my best friend would hate me if she knew. I didn't want her to find out, so I pretended everything was fine. I was getting to be an expert actress. We hung out together for the rest of the day. I never wanted to go home.

Chapter 4: Family Legacy

Fathers, do not provoke or irritate or fret your children
[do not be hard on them or harass them], lest they
become discouraged and sullen and morose and feel
inferior and frustrated (Colossians 3:21).

A fter that dreadful day, I made sure I was never alone with my father.

I have come to believe he was a very sick man, possibly bipolar, like me. It's my firm belief his drinking was his attempt to self-medicate. I have learned a lot in the ensuing years and have finally been able to forgive him. He died alone from cirrhosis of the liver—a slow, messy, agonizing death. It is my hope that in his last hours he reached out to God for forgiveness. It is my prayer the same grace that covers all my sins covers his, and I will see him one day, redeemed in heaven. Why? Because like many abusers, my father was a victim of his father. He was also an alcoholic pedophile. It's impossible to know how many generations ago this all began.

I've heard it said the things some people condemn the loudest are the things they are secretly guilty of doing themselves. This was the case later that same summer. One evening, at a rented cottage, my grandfather committed his own unspeakable crime against my cousin and me. What I experienced that night actually became the beginning of the end of the sexual abuse by my father.

35

But I Liked It...and Other Lies

My grandparents moved from Michigan to southern California in the early sixties. Every couple of years after their move they would come back for a week or two to visit. That summer, they rented a cottage at a nearby lake so all the various relatives could call on them at one place, thus saving them the hassle of driving all over the county.

That day, some of my father's cousins were out at the lake when my family was there. One of them had a daughter just a year younger than me. On the rare occasions we were together, we always got along famously. It was decided we would both spend the night at the cottage and have all the next day to be together. We could swim, sunbathe, and do all the things any two teenage girls would do to have fun. It was the kind of adventure I didn't often get to experience, and I was thrilled.

We spent the evening playing cards and getting hugs. There was some drinking, but my father and grandfather out-drank everyone else, as usual. Later on in the night, my grandfather crept into the room my cousin and I were sharing and molested first me and then her. I pretended to be asleep during both assaults. He kept repeating, "Don't tell your father."

When he was finished, he turned out the light. (Yes, he had the audacity to turn on the light.) He left the room, leaving behind a familiar, disturbing scent that mingled with the mustiness of the small cottage room and turned my stomach. My poor cousin was devastated. Shaking and sobbing, she climbed into my bed. She had never experienced anything like this.

While my cousin was understandably frightened, my guilt once again rose to the surface. *Was this my fault too?* My mind reeled, filling with self-blame. I told myself I was guilty: guilty about the hugs that may have led to this; guilty I hadn't protected her; guilty because I pretended to sleep while she cried. I also felt guilty that *I* wasn't crying. I hated what had happened, but for me it was minor compared to what my father had done. It wasn't minor, however; it was appalling. It was also her first encounter with this sort of evil, and she needed comfort and support. All she received from me, though, was the vain repetition that I was asleep and couldn't remember anything. To my shame, I told her I had no idea what she was talking about. I felt horrible but still I did nothing. Guilty.

The next morning we came out of the bedroom to find my grandfather sitting at the breakfast table, cheerfully drinking coffee and eating. To all outward appearances, he and my grandmother presented the perfect happy family picture. My cousin and I quickly said our good mornings, skirted the kitchen, and went directly outside. She immediately insisted she wanted to call her parents. Panic overwhelmed me. Though I told her over and over we just couldn't, she would not be swayed. There wasn't a phone at the cottage, so we made our way to the manager's office some distance away. By the time we arrived, my cousin was sobbing uncontrollably. She managed to make her request understood, however, and the sweet older couple who managed the cottages didn't hesitate to let her use their phone. Through her tears, she told her mother Grandpa had hurt us in the night, and she wanted to come home. Unbeknownst to me, her mother called my parents, the result being they all descended upon the cottage to confront my grandfather.

We hadn't gone back to the cottage, but had waited around for her parents to arrive. In our naïve minds, we thought her parents would just come, pick her up, and I could ride home with them. It had never occurred to us that her parents would want to confront our grandfather. It certainly had not crossed our minds they would call *my* parents. When we saw both cars pull up and our angry parents spill out and head for the cottage, we were frightened. We approached the cottage, but didn't go in. We could hear the angry shouting; to my surprise, the loudest shouting came from my father. He was furious, swearing and accusing his father of being foul, perverted, and evil. As I heard this through the window, my mind seized up, unable to comprehend such hypocrisy coming from my father's mouth. All the way home, he ranted to my mother while I just sat in the back seat, listening, totally confused, and thinking all the while, *This is insane!* From that day forward, no amount of convincing would allow me to think the things I did with my father were out of love. My eyes were opened now. All of this was perverted and evil; my father's own words had convicted him. I felt perverted and evil for going along with it. Deep within myself, I had to have known it was wrong, but I forced the knowledge out of the reach of my conscious mind. I wouldn't allow myself to go there. This clinched it. After this, I couldn't help but go there. This truly was the beginning of the end.

Chapter 5: Dark Times

For we do not want you to be uninformed, brethren, about the affliction and oppressing distress which befell us...how we were so utterly and unbearable weighed down and crushed that we despaired even of life [itself] (2 Corinthians 1:8).

T hen something happened that sickened me with guilt, yet in the end brought me the courage to do what needed to be done.

I had been to a neighborhood dance and had come home late, but in a good mood, expecting everyone to be asleep. My mood came crashing down when I saw my father sitting in his chair, watching TV in the otherwise darkened house. He was obviously waiting up for me. When he saw me, he called me to come over and sit by him.

Weakly, I told him no. He wouldn't let it go, and I found myself drifting over to the chair as I had so many times before. This time though, I only sat on the arm of the chair, with my back to him. I was wearing a dress and had on a girdle with garters and nylons. Somehow I felt impregnable with all of this on. He began to rub my back. It felt so good; it broke down all my firm, carefully constructed resolutions to resist. It had been months since the last time anything happened. I gave in to the moment and allowed him to bring me to climax, despite my promise to myself to never let it happen again.

But I Liked It...and Other Lies

Immediately I was overcome with shame and self-reproach. When it was over I pushed his hand away and walked quickly to the stairs. I wanted to get as far away from him as possible. From behind me, I heard him drunkenly demand that I go up to my room and return to the couch, wearing only a nightgown and nothing else. If I obeyed him this time, I knew where it would lead. Even though it felt selfish to do so, I quietly said, "No."

Startled at my refusal, he became angry, loudly repeating his demand. Again I said, "No," this time with a little more force.

By now furious, he shouted, "Get upstairs, get undressed, and come back down!"

This time I yelled as loud as I could, "No!" I wanted someone to hear us and wake up. I was disappointed when no one did. He must've been scared that someone would, though, because instead of shouting back, he just looked at me with loathing.

I fled to my room, unable to cry for the disgust I felt at myself for having given in to him again. I'd felt pleasure. I was sick with humiliation and guilt. I was so conditioned to saying yes; I even felt I was self-indulgent for *not* doing what was expected. Ashamed.

Another lovely Saturday morning was here, but I stayed in bed as long as possible. I didn't want to face the day. Filled with revulsion at what I believed I'd become—self-centered and weak. No matter how much I hated to do it, I had to get up eventually. When I did, I found my mother waiting for me. She had heard all the yelling the night before after all, and now wanted to know what it was all about. I found myself upset and thought, *She heard the yelling and didn't get up?*

40

Roxanne Fawley

Nevertheless, I had a decision to make. What was I to tell her? A lie? The truth? Telling her the whole truth was definitely not an option. I was terrified at the very thought, because my father had told me many times what would happen if I ever told her about us. He always said he would tell her I came on to him. He would say I enjoyed it. My stomach clenched with panic. I just quietly told her that Dad had tried to get fresh with me. I'd heard the term "fresh" from somewhere, and it just popped into my head.

I was shocked when she believed *me* and became angry at *him*. I was not at all prepared for this reaction, though I was grateful.

It's horrible to even imagine, but many girls are not believed by their mothers. I am grateful for the fact that it wasn't like that in my case.

She stormed into their bedroom, yelling at my father. This woke him from a dead sleep. He was hung over, and in the beginning still in a stupor. When it began to sink in what she was accusing him of, he blamed me for everything. This was just as I'd expected. He said I'd teased him, asked for it, and liked it. He didn't know I'd only said he *tried* to get fresh. He thought she knew everything.

It wasn't long before I found out my mother wasn't surprised he was a molester. She *knew* he had molested three neighborhood girls, because they had told her. She was shocked, however, to find that he was capable of trying to be carnal with his own daughter.

My mind was whirling with questions. She believes me? This happened before? Is it really going to be over, just like this? She isn't going to believe him, even though some of it's true? Relief! Yet, I was full of fear, blame, and shame. Fear of

41

what I thought was the truth coming out, and shame. Always shame. Why blame? I had not been completely truthful. I was believed for a half truth. Though my mother wasn't buying any of what my father was saying, *I* still believed it was true. So true, I wondered if I could trust myself not to go back for more.

That's when I came up with the abhorrent idea I would do for myself what he'd always done. It was the beginning of years of self-abuse and mental torture. Being brainwashed, so to speak, I had to think of him and what we'd done for anything to happen. Because of this, I relived the first time over and over and over. I hated myself more each time. I felt evil. I thought I deserved to die. I mistakenly believed it was the only way I would ever stop.

Such thoughts of suicide were not new to me. Some of my earliest memories were of wanting to die. Most four year olds drift off to sleep with thoughts of toys or memories of the games they played during the day. When they are fortunate, they think of their parents and smile as dreams claim them. When I was four, I remember lying in the dark, thinking of ways I could die. It comforted me to think of slipping away into the dark, never waking to face another day. Suicidal thinking somehow became my favorite solution to everything wrong in my world. This thought pattern would continue to plague me until my mid-fifties.

One year on Halloween, when I was still four, I made my first attempt at carrying out these suicidal thoughts. I'd been sick and unable to go trick or treating. I listened as my brother and sister came home, bragging about the enormous haul of candy they'd gotten from our generous neighbors. A half-formed idea was already brewing in my mind. After everyone was asleep, I quietly crept downstairs to the living room. Sure enough, there on the coffee table were two big bowls of candy. It was irresistible, especially to a child who had been ill and not eating well for a few days. I was hungry. I only planned to eat a little from each bowl. Before long, every bit of candy was gone, and I was staring at two empty bowls.

I shivered as the realization hit me. The consequences would be awful when the empty bowls were discovered in the morning. Then I remembered my mother's admonition earlier in the day, when she had doled out a single orange baby aspirin to me. "Remember, Roxanne, this is *not* candy; it's medicine. If you take too many, it could kill you! So never take medicine unless I give it to you."

Here was my answer! Since my mother had never dreamed I would disobey her, the bottle with the remaining baby aspirins was on the kitchen counter, easily within my reach. No childproof bottles in those days. I simply removed the top and ate them like I had the candy. It didn't take me long to finish off the entire bottle of baby aspirin. They began to get bitter toward the end, but I was determined. I then went back up to bed and waited to die.

I awoke to a loud commotion downstairs. Kathy was sobbing, Marty was yelling, and I (much to my consternation) was inexplicably still alive. My mother hollered up the stairs, "Roxanne Moran, get down here right now!" while in the background I heard Marty feeding her a nonstop stream of suggestions for creative punishments to be inflicted upon me. When I got down to the living room, Marty focused his wrath on me. Kathy was still crying, heartbroken that her beloved candy was gone. My mother stepped between Marty and me, taking charge of the situation before he could administer his own justice. She ordered me to the kitchen, then headed to the nail on the wall where the flyswatter was kept. This was her go-to instrument of discipline. Her progress across the kitchen halted however, when her eyes fell upon the empty aspirin bottle.

She turned and stared at me, aghast. "You *ate* the aspirin after I told you not to? Wasn't the candy enough for you? Now we're going to have to take you to the hospital and get your stomach pumped." There was no sympathy in her voice whatsoever. She obviously misunderstood what I had done, thinking I had merely eaten the aspirin like candy, after all.

It never occurred to me to tell her the truth. My mind was busy with the thought of having my stomach pumped. I had no idea what it meant, but it didn't sound good to me. It wasn't. It took four adults to hold me down in the emergency room as they put the tubing down my nose. I wish I could say it was the last time in my life this ever happened.

One snowy day a few years later when I was seven, I was playing outside and not wanting to ever go home—as usual. This time, though, I decided to do something about it. I had heard that when people froze to death, they just fell asleep. I thought how nice it would be, to fall asleep in the snow and never wake up. I made up my mind this was what I would do. I lay back in the snow, looked up at the sun, and closed my eyes. I grew very sleepy. I tried to *go* to sleep, but the urge to urinate became so intense I was afraid I would wet myself. Ironically, I was much more afraid of what my parents would do if I did, that I got up from the snowbank and went home to use the bathroom.

Given all the circumstances, by the time I was fourteen, my life had become one long nightmare. I was cast into such a deep depression I felt I had no choice *but* to die. One night when everyone was sleeping, I got out of bed and went down to the bathroom where my mother kept all our medicine. There were two large bottles of adult aspirin in the cupboard. I'd read on the bottle you weren't supposed to exceed six pills in a 24-hour period. I was certain this time that taking both bottles would kill me. I went to the kitchen, reached for a glass, filled it with water and began swallowing aspirin by the handful. I didn't stop until both bottles were empty. Feeling peaceful and oddly content, I went upstairs to my bed to sleep, positive I'd never wake up.

Wake I did though, to wave after wave of nausea. I rushed downstairs to the bathroom only to empty my stomach of all the aspirin I had so painstakingly ingested just a few short hours ago. As my parents' bedroom was right next to the bathroom, they must have heard me. I was not surprised when in the morning my mom asked me how I was feeling. By now I was finished with vomiting, but I had a loud ringing in my ears, so I told her about it. Ever since my brush with death, when I'd had hepatitis, she was much more concerned when any of us were sick. Unable to go to our family doctor because it was a Saturday, she whisked me off to the ER. The doctor on call quickly picked up on the symptoms and figured out I had overdosed on aspirin. When he asked me if this was what I'd done, I lied (again); I was terrified by what my mother's reaction to the truth would be. It never even crossed my mind that telling the truth could have gotten me the help I desperately needed. If only I'd been honest. To this day I still wonder how it was possible my mom never missed the aspirin.

There were so many other clues that I was broken and confused. Always a storyteller, I made up completely untrue stories and would share them with my elderly friends in the neighborhood. There was old Jonesy, Mr. and Mrs. Slater, and Mrs. Stonerock.

My siblings always kidded me that the stork brought me to the wrong house. I was meant to go next door where my name would have been Roxanne Stonerock! My dear old friends would pump me for information about my home life and fill me with cookies for entertaining them. I never disappointed them. I would tell the most outlandish tales, all happy ones. Sometimes they would ask me what I wanted to be when I grew up, just to hear me say, "A nun or a stripper!" How they would laugh. How sad is that? I was either going to be all pure or all sexual even at this young age. Nothing in between. Black or white. What a prediction for a bipolar disorder, which I have been diagnosed with.

I have a chemical imbalance which causes manic depression. I have situational depression as well. I take medicine for the one and have received years of counseling for the other. I was either extremely high or terribly low. Unfortunately for me, I had fewer manic episodes than depressed ones. Mania can sometimes be enjoyable. I'd be funny, more creative, and full of energy.

Something as simple as going on a diet could start me off into a manic state of mind, especially if diet pills were involved. When I was manic, I thought I was the smartest, most beautiful and talented person in the world. I could go without sleep, and often would, preferring instead to clean my whole house. Even the drawers would get organized. Then I would shop. Oh, how I could shop! I would redecorate the house a hundred different ways, all in my mind. I oozed creativity.

Roxanne Fawley

Something as trivial as gaining a little bit of weight could cause me to slide into a depression. Other times it would be a bad memory that would trigger an episode. When I was depressed, I wanted to sleep all the time. I couldn't be creative if my life depended on it. The house would get dusty, the laundry would pile up, and no meals would get made. It was a self-perpetuating cycle. I would feel so worthless. Then I would look around at the house and feel even more worthless. I remember thinking "sh*t" had more value, because at least *it* could be used as fertilizer.

This is only a little glimpse into what it's like to be bipolar. One day on a glorious mountaintop, the next day in a dark, dank pit. All or nothing—literally.

Chapter 6: Tom

A good man eats good from the fruit of his mouth, but the
desire of the treacherous is for violence (Proverbs 13:2).

I met my husband, Tom, when I was just sixteen. The boy
who'd been my friend for the last two years had just
broken up with me and I was distraught. I'd met him when
I was fourteen and thought we would marry one day. I was
as depressed as only a brokenhearted sixteen year old can be.
I shut myself in my bedroom and cried for a whole week.
My best friend, Lois, was now eighteen with a job and her
own car. It was a brand new 1970 blue muscle car. She finally
succeeded in getting me to leave my room on a hot June day
by saying she needed me. She wanted to take me to a car wash
business where a guy she knew worked. He in turn knew the
guy she was interested in. She wanted me to ask the car wash
guy if the other guy liked her. Tom was the car wash guy.

When we arrived at the car wash, Lois pointed Tom out.
He was 5 feet 10 inches and thin, with sandy hair and freckles.
It was my job to approach him and ask if this other boy liked
Lois.

"Why? Does she like him?" he asked in return.

"Why should I tell you that if you don't even know?" I
replied.

Then he said, "That makes sense!"

But I Liked It...and Other Lies

Well, no one had ever said I made sense before. I'd always had a ditzy blonde personality of sorts, even though I was a brunette. So naturally I was instantly smitten with him for saying that. I returned to Lois' car, got in, and told her she was indeed liked by her guy. At the same time, I wanted to know, "Who was this other guy?"

"Oh, Roxanne! He's Tom Fawley, and you don't want to start liking him!" She went on to say, "He never dates the same girl twice!"

"I'm going to marry him!" I told her. Sure enough, two years later she was our maid of honor.

Tom was quiet and handsome. One of my cousins said he looked like a young Steve McQueen. He had blue eyes and pale skin, with very small ears. My mom always said my *dad's* ears made him look like a taxicab with the doors open. So I would notice a thing like this.

There was an annual fireworks show at a local high school football field for the Fourth of July. In a spur of the moment decision, a group of us decided to get together and go. Once there, Tom and I happened to (accidentally on purpose) pair up. It was a hot, perfect midsummer evening. A few of us decided we just couldn't stand to see it end so soon. West Lake was only a short distance away, so swimming was chosen as a way to prolong the fun. In the dark, under the stars, I couldn't resist flirting with Tom. Just before the evening came to an end, Tom slipped up next to me in the water and kissed me. I awoke the next morning, still reliving the entire evening, and waited for Tom to call. I was still waiting weeks later. Angry at myself for allowing that kiss, I had resigned myself to the fact Lois had been right.

Roxanne Fawley

Finally giving up on ever hearing from Tom, I went on with my summer. I was invited to stay up north for a week at a friend's cottage, and that's where I was when Lois excitedly called me. She had found out through the grapevine Tom intended to ask me out the next Friday. Knowing I wasn't going to be back until Saturday, she got directions from my friend's parents, then drove up to get me. What a friend! She made certain I was home for his phone call.

Sure enough, he called at 7:30 p.m. Friday to ask me out to a drive-in movie the same night. Of course I said yes. I spent the next two hours getting ready for our first date.

When Tom came to pick me up, he saw my father passed out in his chair in the living room. He was wearing only white boxers, and had two broken arms. (The reason for which I will explain later in my story.)

I could tell Tom didn't know what to think or say, so we just left for the movies. When we arrived at the drive-in, he parked his car right next to Lois' car. Tom was driving a light blue 1963 sporty looking car. He had been very quiet up until this time, but now asked if I wanted some popcorn.

"Yes, thank you," I said.

He then told me to roll down my car window and motioned for Lois to roll down hers. He leaned across me, yelling to her, "You want some popcorn?"

Shocked at his thoughtfulness, she answered, "Why, yes, Tom!"

He then answered her with, "Go take Roxanne and get some!"

We were both taken aback. How rude!

51

But I Liked It...and Other Lies

During the movie, I started to say something to him, but he interrupted me with, "Two bucks a head, watch the movie." I was flabbergasted, and yet inexplicably in love.

In the past, I would always tire of a boy if he showed genuine interest in me. All except my first love, which was a very immature on-and-off-again relationship. I'd like him; he'd like me. He wouldn't like me, so I wouldn't like him. So childish. We broke up many times in the two years we were together. We didn't really date; we were too young. We just hung out together at the playground near my house in Oakwood. In the summer, we would go swimming. We would walk all over the neighborhood, holding hands and talking. We really loved each other, as much as we could for our ages (fourteen till sixteen). We were both messed up kids from dysfunctional families. It's probably what drew us together in the first place, even if we didn't know it at the time. His father was also an alcoholic.

Tom, on the other hand, came from a very loving, stable home. He had a father and mother who loved each other, and five brothers and sisters. I just couldn't tell if he liked me! My mother always said that he must've read the book on how to keep me interested.

He kept asking me out about two hours before picking me up. I would spend the whole day getting ready in anticipation of his call. We dated three Fridays in a row. On the fourth Friday the phone didn't ring. I was in the dark as to why. There I was, all ready, with no place to go.

At the time all this took place, I worked at the root beer stand in Milwood. Lois and my sister, Kathy, worked there with me, along with a couple of other girls.

Roxanne Fawley

Around 9:00 p.m., Lois stopped by. Knowing I must be miserable, she wanted me to hear from her why Tom hadn't called. She had been at a party, and seen Tom there with one of our coworkers.

I was angry at the girl, and hurt that she would go out with him and do that to me, but Lois came to her defense. She said that when Tom approached this girl to hang out with her at the party, she had (to her credit) asked, "What about Roxanne?"

Lois then proceeded to tell me how Tom had answered.

She'd heard him say, "She asks too many stupid questions." (I was only trying to get him to talk.)

"She's too forward." (All I did was kind of lean his way in case he wanted to put an arm around me or hold my hand.)

Finally: "She won't even let me leave when the date's over." (I just wasn't in a hurry to go into the house and face my drunken father's questions and accusations.)

Now I was mad at *him*! He could just see if I'd ever go out with him again.

The next Friday was *not* spent getting ready for a date. Instead, I played softball in the August heat in my bare feet. I was sweaty and filthy. But Tom did call. I took the call, but with quiet indifference instead of my usual talkative self. I merely answered his questions with a "yes" or "no."

He asked if something was wrong and I answered with a very icy, "No." He asked if I wanted to see a movie, but instead of quickly saying yes, I uncharacteristically asked, "What's playing?"

I did end up saying I'd go. I didn't do one thing to get ready, however. I didn't brush my hair or my teeth. I didn't wash my face or feet. I didn't even change my dirty sweaty clothes! But what did he do when he saw me? He gave me my first compliment and said I looked nice. Humph! When I thought about all the hours I used to spend getting ready, it made me boil. I was a hot mess and he *dared* to say I looked nice? I must have looked mad because once again he asked me if something was wrong. Once again I answered with a clipped, "No."

This time when I got into his car, I hugged the passenger side door and didn't say a word. Again, "What's the matter?"

Again, "Nothing." I spent the movie leaning against the door, never speaking a word. He was bewildered, obviously out of his element with this new Roxanne.

When he brought me home, I quickly got out of his car and started walking toward my house.

He jumped out and shouted, "Something is too wrong!"

I calmly turned and faced him. I matter-of-factly said, "Only if you think I ask too many stupid questions, am too forward, and don't let you leave when you want to."

I fully expected him to deny saying those things, and that would be the end of it. He'd be a liar and we would be over.

To my surprise, he said, "I said those things, but I didn't mean them. I was starting to care for you and it scared me."

I thought, *What's this? The truth?* I wasn't prepared for that. I melted into his arms, thinking, *A truthful man.* All was right with my world for that moment. He cared about me, and for the first time it didn't put me off to have someone genuinely care. Would wonders never cease? I was in love.

Six months went by and we were invited to go to a New Year's Eve party. When Tom came into my house to pick me up, he started talking to my mom and didn't hear my father's drunken, "Happy New Year!" All of a sudden, Dad yelled, "Well, screw you!" Once again, Tom had no idea what to do or say, so taking me by the hand, we just quickly left.

When we arrived at the party, Tom left me with some people and then he disappeared. Disturbed, I thought to myself things were probably over between us. I was sure Tom had had enough of the drama with my dad, and didn't even want to try and deal with it anymore. It was practically midnight before I finally saw him again. He just walked up to me and took me into a quiet, empty bedroom, took my face in his hands, and tenderly kissed me. "I'm going to marry you," was all he said.

It wasn't a question. It was more like a fact. I was elated! *When?* I wondered to myself. I couldn't wait to be free from my home life, and immediately started making plans in my head. Imagine my dismay when the castles I created in the air came crashing down as months went by, and Tom never even mentioned it again.

During this time I was blessed to be living with my Grandmother Jungel and going to school my senior year in Lawrence, Michigan. Unfortunately, I still had to come home on weekends if I wanted to spend time with Tom. Those weekends at home were never pleasant.

Chapter 7: Meltdown

For out of the heart come evil thoughts (reasoning's and disputings and designs) such as murder, adultery, sexual vice... (Matthew 15:19).

My days as my father's precious Roxannie were forgotten history. I was now an evil seductress who had ruined his marriage. He kept blaming all the turmoil between my mother and him on me and constantly berated me when I was present. That left me feeling unsure of myself and unwelcome in my own home.

I thought the sexual abuse with my father was over, but it merely deteriorated into something just as sinister.

One Saturday afternoon I was home and getting ready for a date with Tom. I needed to take a bath and wash my hair, but no one else was home and that always worried me. My father was sleeping—passed out in his chair, so I cautiously went into the bathroom and soundlessly closed the door. It was a firm rule in our house of six people to never lock the bathroom door just in case someone needed to use the toilet. I filled the tub with water and bubble bath and slipped into the water. When I lay back to get my hair wet I heard a strange noise coming from behind the faucet. With a sickening feeling in the pit of my stomach I slowly sat up and looked into a hole that was in the wall next to the faucet and saw my dad's eye looking back at me! I froze. I literally could not move. I couldn't breathe. My heart pounded so fast and hard I was afraid he would hear it. We just stared, eye to eye, for what seemed like an eternity, though it was probably only a minute or two. Finally his eye withdrew and he slid a board back over the hole. I was in shock, still unable to move. I have no idea how much time had passed. Still trembling, I thought, *How long had this been going on? Was this the first time?* I eventually was able to breathe and move. Without even bothering to rinse off, I now couldn't move fast enough! I jumped out of the soapy water and into my clothes and peeked out the door. My dad still looked as though he was asleep. Was I losing my mind? I crept past him and went next door to a neighbor's house. I don't remember what I said to them. I think I merely asked if I could stay there until my mother came home. I was visibly upset and still soapy. They let me, and thankfully they didn't ask me any questions.

When my mom came home from the grocery store, I went home and told her what had happened. This started another furiously emotional exchange of harsh words; hers accusing, his excusing. My mother called my father a sick pervert, and a few other defaming things. He whined; he was only looking for his keys on the floor. Neither one of us believed it. Not for a split second!

All I knew was how I felt—violated and afraid to be in my own home. You'd think I would be used to it by then, but in a way I can only try to explain, it almost felt worse than being molested. Then, I at least *thought* I had *some* control. Now, I felt completely helpless. In my thoughts, I relived the past and agonized about my future. I blamed myself for ever having tried to take a bath without my mother or anyone else at home, saying to myself, *You should've realized he wasn't really sleeping.*

58

Roxanne Fawley

These things continued to happen whenever I came home for the weekend. One time, I just looked out the window, waiting for Tom to come and pick me up for our date, when my father hollered, "Get away from that window! You're acting like a dog in heat!" He, of course, assumed I was sexually active. I wasn't. Not in the way he thought anyway.

There was another horrible incident that took place when I was home. It was another hot, muggy June day. In spite of the heat, I was wearing a floor length, high necked, long sleeved, white quilted robe Lois had given me for Christmas. I always wore it when I was home, no matter how hot it was, because I wanted to be completely covered up. On this particular day, I had to walk past my father, who was sitting in his chair, on my way to the bathroom. I had already bathed when my mother was home, but she was gone now, and I had to use the toilet. He stared maliciously at me as I walked by. Then before I knew what was happening, he leaped out of his chair and walked up close to me, drunkenly spewing accusations that I was teasing him. *Me?* How was it even possible? I was wearing a long robe, no makeup, and had curlers in my hair! He started trying to undo my robe. I got so scared I grabbed a big decorative wooden spoon hanging on the wall beside me. I intended to hit him with it, but instead he grabbed it out of my hand and hit me in the head. It only hurt a little, because of the curlers in my hair, but I just lost it anyway! I went out of control, yelling at him and hitting him with my fists. He actually looked scared as I backed him into their bedroom and pushed him against the wall. I kept pounding on him and yelling. I wasn't going to stop until he was dead and he knew it.

He started to yell, "Help! She's trying to kill me!"

But I Liked It...and Other Lies

My younger brother who was only thirteen at the time came home right then and got mad at *me*! He pulled me off our dad and yelled, "Why do you even bother to come home if you're just going to cause trouble?" He had no idea what I had been through with Dad and just wanted some semblance of peace in his home.

I ran upstairs, crying hysterically. My thoughts were a scrambled mess. I wasn't trying to tease him, was I? Would I really have killed him? How could a fully robed person in curlers, with no makeup, be a tease? I went to my bedroom and looked in my mirror. My tearful face disgusted me. I hated what I saw. This time though, I had no bruise to show for what had just happened. It didn't seem right to hurt so bad and have nothing to show for it. I picked up my fancy, sterling silver hairbrush I'd bought with my babysitting money, and hit myself in the face. It felt wonderful! I hit my face again and again, harder and harder until I had a gruesome bruise on my cheek and eye. The whole side of my face was on fire and I felt gratified. I stopped when my brother came upstairs to yell at me some more, but when he saw the bruise, instead he asked, "He did that to you?"

I didn't answer. He ran down the stairs and let loose all his disgust toward Dad for being a drunken bully and picking on a girl. I was glad he was no longer mad at me, but once again it wasn't the whole truth. Not about the bruise, anyway. More lies. More guilt and shame.

I had found a new coping skill, though. From then on, whenever the hurt I felt inside would become unbearable, I just had to hit myself *hard* and I would feel a strange release.

Tom didn't like to be seen with me if I had bruises, and I didn't like having to invent excuses for them. I began to hit myself in the head till it hurt, but only in places where nothing could show.

I continued this habit of hurting myself to get relief from emotional pain until my mid-fifties.

After I was married, we had purchased a large rubber mallet to clean our carpets. We sprayed the carpet cleaner on the spot and then covered it with a cloth and pounded it with the mallet until the stain came out. It worked wonders. But *I* used it to hurt myself. I would hit myself in the head until I'd almost pass out. Nevertheless, it never broke the skin. Sometimes, I would beat myself in the stomach and chest and found that I gleaned a sick comfort from the bruises only I would see. It bothered me that my emotional pain was invisible. Ugly, purple welts gratified me in a way I can't explain.

This sort of behavior is often seen in people with borderline personality disorder. I've learned that people who suffer from BPD tend to view people as either all good or all bad. They can have fluctuating, quick-as-a-blink mood swings. My own fear of being alone coupled with self hatred tended to make Tom feel like he was walking in a mine field. Many people with this disorder cut themselves until they bleed, but I never wanted to leave a mark the world could see after that first time.

When I was in my mid-fifties, I entered a program at Interact of Michigan called DBT (dialectical behavioral therapy). I had to commit to one year of one-on-one counseling once a week. I had two hours per week of group therapy, and I had access to twenty-four hours a day life coaching. I had to promise to call coaching if I had any urges of self-harm so they could encourage me to use alternate ways of coping, utilizing the skills I learned in therapy. There were twenty-nine skills in all. My personal favorites included the following: Nonjudgmental

Stance, toward self or others; Urge Surf, avoid acting on a temporary urge, it will pass; and, Act Opposite to Current Emotion. I really liked, but more importantly used, all twenty-nine tools.

There was also a DBT Diary Card. On it, I would daily rate my urges and emotions on a scale of zero to five. Zero meant the least and five the most. I still use that scale today. Zero was good if I was rating self-harm thoughts or anger, but five was best when rating Joy. Other emotions to be rated were Sadness, Fear, Shame, Guilt, and Misery. Depending on the ratings, I would then apply the DBT skills needed to cope with the different emotions and what caused them. There was also a place on the Diary Card to write about important events of each day that I could then cover in counseling or class.

God blessed DBT and used it to save my life and marriage. Unfortunately, I didn't learn about it until I was fifty-four. I've highly recommended it to others who have shared their troubled stories with me and are bipolar or who are suffering from suicidal thoughts or borderline personality disorders.

Up until the time I'd enrolled in DBT, I'd been hospitalized for severe depression at least once a year from my late twenties on. In my late thirties I began receiving countless ECT treatments (electrical convulsive therapy), better known as shock treatments. My medicines and counseling were not working, and we were desperate and ready to try anything. I continued to undergo these treatments on and off until I was well into my fifties. Did they work? I'm not really certain. I am still here, though. I will be completely honest now and admit I really submitted myself to them with the hope they would kill me. There is a risk of death any time you have general anesthesia administered, and I was desperate to die without committing suicide. Even though I had succumbed to despair and attempted it a few times, I never wanted or meant to subject my family to that kind of devastating grief.

Wanting to die, even when not actively planning to take your life, is called suicidal ideation. It's a miserable way to exist.

Looking back, I think my father suffered from suicidal tendencies. On more than one occasion I remember him holding his wrist over a wastebasket and cutting at it halfheartedly with a razor. I recall one particular time he actually begged Kevin and me to help him. Of course my mother wouldn't let us, although she wasn't about to stop him. And then, there *is* the fact that he did take his own life, when all was said and done.

Chapter 8: Burden of Guilt

O God, You know my folly and blundering; my sins
and my guilt are not hidden from You (Psalm 69:5).

By the time my father was forty-five, his life had done a complete reversal. No longer was he the powerful domineering tyrant, holding the family under his brutal thumb. His appearance was so altered that at first glance a stranger would take this shriveled shell of a man to be in his mid-seventies. A combination of the years of abusing alcohol and a poor genetic history had caused him to develop cirrhosis of the liver. (His grandmother had died of cirrhosis without ever having had a drink in her life.)

My mother eventually came to realize she had nothing to fear from the feeble man he had become and told him he had to leave. She proceeded to file for divorce, while he lived alone in an apartment. When my father was younger and stronger, she had tried to leave him four times. In every instance, he threatened to kill her, and all of us children, too. She really believed he was capable of it, and looking back, I know he was.

By this time, his condition had deteriorated to the point where he was vomiting blood every time he drank. Tom and I had rescued him twice from bleeding to death. He had been hospitalized both times for losing huge amounts of blood. Our doctor had finally told him not to come to him if he ever chose to take another drink; he had better things to do than waste his time on someone intent on killing himself.

My father eventually started going to AA meetings in the vain hope that my mother would take him back. He was sober for a period of about six months prior to the event that would lead to his death.

It was a Thursday afternoon when our telephone rang. I picked it up to hear my father on the other end. I was surprised to hear his voice; after all, I hadn't spoken to him since my mom insisted he leave. Sounding...*hopeful?* He said, "I saw in the paper you're getting married. So, where do I rent my tux?"

I was getting married to Tom on July 14, 1972, just three months away. My engagement picture had been in the local newspaper; but in the announcement I submitted, I had purposely left out his name, as if I had no father.

I had no idea where my courage came from, but the words poured from me. I told him in no uncertain terms he wasn't to go anywhere. He wasn't even invited to the wedding. This was one special day he was not going to ruin. I also told him he had no right to give me away. Not waiting for a response, I hung up. Shaken by the call, and trembling inside at my own uncharacteristic harshness, I stood by the phone for the longest time. I began to second guess myself. I knew my mother and siblings would be nothing if not relieved to have him absent from the wedding. What about our extended family and friends, though? What about Tom's family? I started imagining the questions I would have to answer and began to feel sick. I wondered if, by protecting myself and my feelings, I was being selfish. I couldn't have him there, though; I just couldn't.

Roxanne Fawley

The next day my father went to work as always, teaching junior high English and US history, apparently acting the same as always. On his way home, he went to a nearby liquor store and wrote his last check, for five bottles of cheap wine. He took them to his lonely, one-bedroom apartment and began drinking. He didn't stop until all that was left was a half-bottle of his purchase. As the doctor had predicted, he violently vomited up blood for the last time. Trails of it were left in every room. He bled to death that night.

He wasn't discovered until the following Monday. When he didn't show up for work, the principal of his school tried to call him, but Dad's phone just rang and rang. Then he tried to reach my mother. She told him she hadn't talked to my dad in more than a week. The principal had warned him if he missed another day of work because of his drinking, it would cost him his job. Though his friend, he'd had enough of covering for him. Angry now at my father, yet dreading what he knew he had to do, he drove to the apartment. Not getting a response to his knocking, he became worried and asked the manager if he would open my dad's place so he could make sure he was all right. When they opened the door, the first thing that hit them was the stench from his bloated body. Later, when they described their first look inside the apartment, they said they thought they were looking at a murder scene because of the amount of blood. This was how my father was found.

My mother said his dying before their divorce was final was the nicest thing he'd ever done for her. As his widow, she would now be able to receive all of his benefits. Our family was relieved. My older brother, Marty, got to come home early from the army; and my younger brother, Kevin, would get to go to college for free. No one in our immediate family, except his mother, grieved his passing. I pretended not to, either.

But I Liked It...and Other Lies

I had been working at my job in a nursing home when I got the news. I was walking by the nurse's station and they said I had a call, and it was my mother. She had never called me at work before. The hairs stood up on my arms.

"Roxanne, George is dead," was all she said. I don't remember what I said, or if I said anything. I do recall going into a patient's room and crying my eyes out. I didn't even know why. Was I sad or were they tears of relief? Or was I feeling guilty? I think of all of them. Of the three, most of all I feared that I was to blame.

He must have wondered how it would look to his family and friends when he wasn't allowed to attend the wedding. Maybe they would even guess the real reason why he wasn't invited. Whatever his thought processes might have been, the next day he was dead, and the newspaper clipping of my engagement picture was found on the table next to his chair. I knew it wasn't a coincidence. I got his message loud and clear. I'd hated him. I had wanted him dead. I wanted him out of my life. I had killed him, but I couldn't tell anyone I thought that or why.

The funeral was awful. The ride to the funeral home must have made the limo driver wonder what kind of unfeeling family we were. All we talked about was the limo, how nice it was, and how the stereo was great. We sat off to the side, out of the sight of people at the funeral. I thought it was so the rest of the guests could not see us smiling and laughing. I realized later funeral homes did this for all families at that time. It was so they could grieve in private.

We were all surprised at the huge turnout. All the teachers and most of his students came. Some even cried. I felt like a

68

freak of nature. I was overwhelmed with so many conflicting emotions.

After the funeral, we returned to the house. Some of the mothers of the children my mom babysat for had put together a lunch, and we celebrated. Mom didn't pretend to grieve, and I respected her for that (even if it was a little embarrassing). I was only too aware that we should be grieving. A normal family would be. But there's the answer. There was nothing normal about our family.

Shortly after the funeral, I tried to break off my engagement to Tom. My sister and her fiancée were planning on having a double wedding with us. She had already broken off her engagement, and I thought I could guess why. We no longer were desperate to leave home. There wasn't a reason any longer. The monster was gone, never to return.

When I tried to break it off with Tom, he unfortunately used the wrong words to dissuade me. The invitations had already been sent, so he said the awful words, "What will people say?"

I saw red. These were the exact words my dad would use to discourage me from telling anyone about our secret. I became so upset with Tom, I was suicidal, wanting to die rather than get married and all it would entail. I believe I let Tom get a glimpse of me at my worst with the hope he would break up with me. He just wrote it off as grief and pre-nuptial jitters.

The week before the wedding Tom and I went to see our priest for counseling. I had gone to this priest my whole life for confession.

When I was fourteen, I had tried to tell him what my father and I were doing. Try to imagine the courage it took to go to a priest with this confession. However, since the age of seven, my confessions had always included the facts that I told lies and had impure thoughts. When I told the priest I was being impure with my father, instead of helping me, he told me not to lie in the confessional. I can't describe the pain I felt when he not only didn't believe me, but worse, accused me of lying! No absolution for me on that dark day.

After talking to both of us for a while, my priest asked to speak with me alone. Tom left the room and my priest proceeded to assure me my father had forgiven *me* before he died.

I found out later the priest had been counseling my father and must have believed my father's lies. He must have sworn to him I had made everything up and ruined his marriage to my mother.

When the priest told me about my father forgiving me, I looked so stricken that he finally realized it had been *me* telling the truth after all. When on our wedding day, he was nowhere to be found, I thought he felt he couldn't in good conscience marry us. I believed he knew I was broken and would be a horrible wife. Looking back now, he probably was too ashamed to face me.

Here it was—our wedding day, and the church was locked. We waited for half an hour. People had started to arrive. I finally went to the rectory and knocked on the door. I waited and waited, not knowing what else to do. Finally someone came and opened the door. They said my priest was out of town! I couldn't comprehend what I was being told. Why, only the Sunday before he had asked me if I was ready for my big day. On top of this, they said there was no record of my wedding being that day, though a different priest had been at my rehearsal the day before. They had to get a substitute priest off of a golf course. Our wedding was about an hour late. The temperature was in the 90s and they had turned off the air conditioning. My hair was a frizzy mess, even though I'd spent the whole day in curlers. Then to add insult to injury, we had to wait to take our wedding pictures until after another girl's wedding rehearsal was over. This made us very late to our own reception.

Weeks later at a church breakfast, my priest came up to me and asked if I'd forgiven him yet. The only thing was, he hadn't said for *what*. For not showing up for our wedding? Or for not believing me?

Roxanne's first communion, age 7

Roxanne at age 14

August, 1968: Roxanne's father George Moran, Roxanne
age 15, sister Kathy age 16, and mother Maxine Moran

Tom and Roxanne on her high school graduation day: June, 1971

Tom and Roxanne's wedding day, July 14, 1972

Tom, Roxanne and Baby Casey: 1976

Tom and Roxanne: 40th Wedding anniversary

Chapter 9: Confusion

In You, oh Lord, do I put my trust and confidently take refuge; let me never be put to shame or confusion (Psalm 71:1).

When I married Tom that July, I weighed 140 pounds. By October, I weighed 160 pounds. The week before my sister's wedding, I had to crash diet on popcorn and coffee just to fit into the matron of honor dress. (Yes, she had decided to get married after all.) I lost ten pounds that week and just barely managed to squeeze into the peach colored dress. Tom had to work the night of the wedding. (I had told him he needed to because we were saving for a down payment on a house, but the truth was I just didn't want him there.) I'm ashamed to say I acted as if I wasn't married and blatantly flirted with one of the groomsmen. He responded in kind by dancing with me and paying a great deal of attention to me. I was frightened by how effortlessly wanton I could be *and* with how the evening could easily have ended, so afterward I ate and gained so much weight that by Christmas I was 180 pounds.

Now, of course, I know I only put on so much weight because I wanted to feel safe again, from myself and what I knew I was capable of. Back then, I had equated being fat with being safe. I came to that conclusion because my father had chosen me for the sexual abuse instead of my older sister.

But I Liked It...and Other Lies

Everything I had ever read on the subject said that it was usually the oldest daughter who was molested. My sister has assured me that nothing of the kind was ever done to her by our dad. So yet again, I wasn't the norm. My sister was standoffish and chubbier than me. That led me to believe that her chubbiness was the reason my father didn't choose her. That belief was why I would put on weight to the point of being obese. I would gain weight to keep away any wanted advances. Yes, I said wanted. Sometimes I would get a crush on a man, and if I was thin I believed he would sense it and be tempted by me. (The only advances I didn't want were my own husband's.) Gaining weight was an attempt on my part to accomplish two things—keep Tom at arm's length, hoping my obese body would be gross to him, and protect me from my own evil desires. Even though I would still get infatuated with other men, I was so heavy that no one could possibly become attracted to me, and this made me feel safe.

I became ashamed of my weight though; I took diet pills and lost 60 pounds by summer. I started to get attention from men again, and I knew it was my own fault, so I gained back all the weight plus more.

I was so confused. I wanted to be thin and pretty, but I *needed* to be fat and safe. All this while, I was still unable to be with Tom intimately without sobbing hysterically. I would want to be with him all day, but the minute he walked through our door I would pick a fight or get my feelings hurt just to keep him away. I loved him, but hated sex. I also hated him sometimes just for wanting to be with me. On the other hand, I was afraid he would get to the point where he would no longer desire to be with me. Confused. Tortured. Like two different people.

76

Roxanne Fawley

I have been diagnosed with dissociative identity disorder, or DID. This is where more than one distinct identity, or personality, exists within the same person. The personalities will "take over" a person depending on various difficult circumstances and without a conscious decision on their part. Dissociative disorders are thought to be mainly brought about by psychological trauma.

I had several personalities that came out under different situations or times of stress. They were me, but at different ages and with different personalities. I would function but not remember things afterward. This sometimes happened during counseling sessions and I would have to be called back to myself. After an episode, Tom or a counselor would tell me what I did or said. I would have trouble believing them. One personality was four years old, one eleven, one fourteen, and another seventeen. Then there was me. All I know for sure is, they all knew me, but I wasn't aware of them until counseling. They hated themselves and wanted me dead. I had to learn to forgive and love myself at every age. They are still with me, but I am aware of them now and sometimes even use their particular strengths to cope with things like pain or fear. I no longer dissociate involuntarily. It's hard to write about what I don't really remember, but my journals do look as though they were written by several different people, each with their own handwriting.

When Tom and I were first married, sex was also physically painful. Our honeymoon was a disaster. I had always been very affectionate with Tom, so he had every reason to expect I would be the same way after we were married. I had never allowed us to go "all the way" because I was a good Catholic girl. Hah! I had insisted we wait until we were married. I'd told him he would be the first. That, at least, was sort of true,

77

as the only thing that had ever entered my vagina were my father's and grandfather's fingers.

To have sex hurt physically somewhat distracted me from the emotional pain. Nevertheless, it was so painful that I went to see a gynecologist to find out the reason. He told me I had a congenital cervix infection. This means I had it from birth, but I know I received it in childhood. This can happen when the cervix is irritated and bacteria causes an infection. As a result, when Tom and I had intercourse, the dormant infection was disturbed, causing severe pain. The doctor said he would have to cauterize my cervix. He also told me it wouldn't hurt.

I drove away, doubled over in pain. I don't know how I made it safely home. I was crying so hard I could barely see!

After a sufficient amount of time had passed and the doctor said I had healed, I still found sex to be physically painful. So I went back to see the doctor. After thoroughly examining me, he said there was no physical reason for it to hurt now and I should probably see a psychiatrist. I was so insulted! I thought he was telling me I was crazy, and it was all in my head. Since there was no physical evidence for my pain, I must be nuts!

Looking back, I know he knew that my infection must have been caused by sexual abuse in my childhood, and I needed counseling. His bedside manner just left something to be desired. When I left his office that late afternoon, it was with physical and mental scars.

Chapter 10: A Baker and the Lord

Jesus Christ, (the Messiah) is [always] the same,
yesterday, today, [yes] and forever (to the ages)
(Hebrews 13:8).

A fter Tom and I were married, I did not trust God with my life. We had stopped going to church. I was bitter and broken. Tom and I both came from Catholic families, but we used the fiasco on our wedding day (our no-show priest) as an excuse to stop attending church.

God had other plans for us, though, and brought a godly man into our lives through a series of divine appointments. Karel Boonzaayer, a bald baker, was to become my second boss and our spiritual father in the most unique way.

I was only seventeen when I graduated from high school. I wanted a full-time job, but no one was hiring full time unless you were eighteen or older. In a last ditch effort, Tom went to his high school guidance counselor. He had been the one who had helped him get him his co-op job while still in school. Tom asked him if there were any jobs for me. The counselor told Tom there was a Dutch baker none of his female students wanted to work for. Tom said, "She'll take it!"

Excited and thankful for the opportunity, I went for an interview with Mr. Boonzaayer. He came out of the back of the bakery wearing all white except for a colorful, frosting-stained apron. The first thing he said to me was, "What religion are you?"

Taken aback, I stammered, "Catholic."

He said, "Good! So am I. What kind of Catholic are you?"

I wondered what he meant by that. Did he mean did I go to Mass regularly or did he wonder which one I attended? There were at least five in the area, so I said, "The church on Kilgore."

"Oh," he said, "Roman Catholic!"

I replied, "Noooooo, I've never been to Rome."

The more he talked, the weirder I thought things became.

After the interview, I had no intention of ever working for this man! I told my mother that if he ever called, asking for me, she was to tell him I already had a job. Another lie.

On August 12th I finally turned 18, and the long summer was over. The trouble was, I still didn't have a job, other than cleaning houses and babysitting.

If you remember back to the 70s, there was usually only one phone per house. Ours was between the dining room and the kitchen. I just happened to be the one walking by when it rang. When I answered it I heard, "Rrrrrocksand Merrran?" (That's Roxanne Moran in a heavy Dutch accent.)

I replied, "Yes?"

He said, "You come in tomorrow morning at 6:30 and I will make a baker out of you!" Click!

I panicked. He didn't even give me a chance to refuse (or lie). I kept poor Tom up until four in the morning crying about not wanting to go to work for this crazy, weird man. Somehow he got me to calm down enough to agree to just give it a try.

After a mere nap, he took me to work two and a half hours later.

And wouldn't you just know I did *everything* wrong. I burned my first batch of fondant (that's a kind of sweet glaze), and then put the new batch on the nice flat bottoms of the éclairs instead of their bumpy tops. Mr. Boonzaayer said he'd assumed I would know the tops from the bottoms.

I told him not to assume anything with me.

After that he put me on a lot of cleaning duties and other tedious jobs, like cracking eggs (hundreds at a time) and folding boxes. I slowly learned other things—like taking cakes out of their pans, cutting them in half, filling them, and frosting them.

This man though—he *loved* his God. He listened to church music and sermons for fun. He read his Bible every day after eating his lunch which he always blessed first. He would literally light up if any customers or friends came into the back room, where we worked, and talked about God. He was a wonderful husband and the loving father of nine children. I still thought he was crazy, but, oh how I wished I could have been one of *his* daughters!

He would ask me questions about my church and beliefs and I wouldn't always know how to answer. Remember at the time all this was happening, I was still unmarried and attended Mass every Sunday. I had also spent eight years in a Catholic school, and had been on the receiving end of hundreds of hours of catechism.

I began approaching the different priests at my church to ask them some of the questions I couldn't answer. For instance, one time I asked one, "What happened at the Council of Trent?"

But I Liked It...and Other Lies

He answered me with the question, "Why on earth would you want to know that?" as if he 1) didn't know the answer, or 2) didn't want to take the time to tell me. Eventually, when they saw me coming toward them, they would quickly run the other way.

It was only natural that I started to ask Mr. Boonzaayer—Karel—questions. He never answered with, "I think..." but always with, "God's Word tells me..." or, "The Bible says...."

I had read prayer books and missals and taken eight years of catechism, but even though we had one at home, I'd never read the Bible.

Karel gave me my first personal Bible. He wrote in it Ephesians 3:16-19. Those are the first verses I ever looked up (with much difficulty, I might add!). They said:

May He grant you out of the rich treasury of His glory to be strengthened and reinforced with mighty power in the inner man by the [Holy] Spirit [Himself indwelling your innermost being and personality]. May Christ through your faith [actually] dwell (settle down, abide, make His permanent home) in your hearts! May you be rooted deep in love and founded securely on love, that you may have the power and be strong to apprehend and grasp with all the saints [God's devoted people, the experience of that love] what is the breadth and length and height and depth [of it]; [that you may really come] to know [practically, through experience for yourselves] the love of Christ, which far surpasses mere knowledge [without experience]; that you may be filled [through all your being] unto all the fullness of God [may have the richest measure of the divine Presence, and become a body wholly filled and flooded with God Himself]!

82

Roxanne Fawley

That was Karel's prayer for me! I loved this man, but I still hated my job, so after the busy Christmas season, I told him I'd taken another job.

I had applied to a nursing home the previous summer, and they had hired me at last!

I thought he'd be glad to be rid of me. I was so out of place with my miniskirts and makeup in such a conservative establishment, and made so many mistakes every day. Everyone else knew their jobs so well. I was truly shocked when he wasn't happy! He gave me a speech so kind it made me cry. Then he gave me a Christmas bonus to boot, and the tears just kept coming. Through sobs that I'm sure made me incoherent, I told him I didn't deserve it and tried to give it back to him. He would have none of it. I left that day in tears and confusion and yet, if I'm to be totally honest, it was a huge relief to be done working there.

I worked for nine months at the nursing home, and saved every penny to spend on our wedding and honeymoon. I worked forty hours a week and got paid every two weeks. I was paying for my wedding by myself and I had saved $800 for this sole purpose. I had also saved $400 for our honeymoon.

Though I loved the residents, I didn't like the way the nursing home was run. There was supposed to be a ratio of six patients to one nurse's aide. We usually had to care for twice that number. I felt like I couldn't do justice to each patient. Some, who didn't have families, were practically neglected. I would spend my fifteen minute breaks doing extra things for my assigned patients like visiting with them, writing letters for them, or doing their hair, but I got called on the carpet for not taking breaks! I couldn't take working there any longer.

But I Liked It...and Other Lies

The day before our wedding was to be my last at that nursing home. I had given them my two weeks' notice.

The day after our wedding, we brought some of our wedding flowers to a few of the residents who didn't normally get visitors. We brought some to a dear patient named Lulu, a spinster with no family. It broke my heart when she responded with, "For me? And it isn't even my birthday." She was crying happy tears.

Once again I found myself out of work in July of 1972. I tried babysitting for two children at our apartment for a while, but it ended when one of them tried to run away! Thank goodness it ended well with the little one safely discovered and returned, but it came as no surprise to me when the parents found someone else to watch over them! Understandably!

October arrived, and I still wasn't employed, but this was all about to change. For a reason known only to God, Tom and I decided to go to a bank branch we had never used before. We always did our banking in Oakwood, nearer to where we were living at the time. This particular bank was in an area called Washington Square. Since we were already in the vicinity we decided we would go there and cash his check. When we got inside, I saw the bald head of my former boss, Karel Boonzaayer.

My first impulse was to turn and run, but since we were already there, I quietly yet frantically said to Tom, "Whatever you do, don't ask Karel how the bakery is doing!"

I knew it was an assiduous time of the year, and his answer would be "busy" with a capital "B." November was fast approaching and Thanksgiving was one of the most intense times of the year. Then I whispered the added warning, "And whatever you do, *don't* let him know I don't have a job!"

Roxanne Fawley

After I was sure I had made myself perfectly clear, we walked up to Karel to say, "Hi," and what comes out of *my* mouth? "How's work?"

Tom shot me a look of astonishment! Karel answered me with, "Yah! We're so busy and I'm short on help!"

And then *I* said, "I don't have a job." Now Tom looked at me with bugged-out eyes like he was thinking, *What are you doing?* I wondered myself! *Who am I? And what did I do with the Roxanne who never wanted to work at the bakery again?*

Karl was so happy with that news; he asked if I could start working the next day.

Just as I had the first time, I kept Tom up until four in the morning, crying about not wanting to go back to work for that weird baker. I couldn't believe how I'd betrayed myself when I said the very things I had pleaded with Tom not to say!

The next morning when I arrived at the bakery, I immediately began to warm up the fondant for the éclairs. Karel was pleased and surprised; I still remembered how. Pleased was a new response from him. During my first stint when I tried to assist there, it seemed like I couldn't do anything right. The last time, I had actually thought I was getting my first compliment from Karl when he said to me, "You know, you never make the same mistake twice." Only then he exclaimed, "But how do you think of so many new ones every day?"

This time my experience at work was different. Instead of noticing everything I did wrong, he was pleasantly commenting on all the things I still remembered how to do correctly; things like setting up the cakes, cutting them, filling them, and frosting them. I had remembered how to remove the cakes from their pans, and how to crack eggs two at a

85

time. I had already known how to clean things, and I simply did so without being told. I had also remembered how to take orders from customers and operate the cash register. Karel was so pleased by all this he began to give me a raise every time I learned a new skill. Especially if they lifted some of his workload. I actually felt like an asset to him for the first time. I started to love working there. I was appreciated! Yes, this time was a completely different work experience for me.

I began again to see Karel as a God-loving, hard-working, family-enjoying, wise man.

One day he quoted from the Bible, saying, "Jesus Christ (the Messiah) is [always] the same, yesterday, today, [yes] and forever (to the ages)" (Hebrews 13:8).

God's own Spirit preached to me from those words the entire weekend. The church I had belonged to had changed so much since I was a child; I never knew for certain where I stood with God. The thought of a God who didn't constantly change the rules appealed to me. This was the beginning of God becoming real to me. Karel patiently, by God's grace, led me to a saving knowledge of Jesus. Two years later he had the privilege of leading Tom to Jesus too! That was the long and the short of it. The man, Karel Boonzaayer, became a spiritual father to both of us.

Chapter 11: Telling Tom

*Hide me from the secret counsel and conspiracy of the
ungodly, from the scheming of evildoers (Psalms 64:2).*

A new roller coaster of events in my life began with an
opportunity to attend a weight loss seminar run by a
local psychologist. During the course of the seminar, he said
sometimes weight gain was subconsciously on purpose, even
protective in a sense. In such cases, the person was afraid
to lose it. I felt as though a light had come on inside; this
explained so much to me.

Afterward, I thanked him for the seminar and told him I
was one of those people he described. No matter how much
I wanted to be thin, I became frightened whenever I began to
succeed at losing weight. He asked if I had to leave right away,
or could we go somewhere to continue our conversation.

We walked to my car; it was the only place I could think
of where we could talk privately. After we had been talking
for only a short while, he told me I had been sexually abused.
He didn't ask me if I had been; he told me I had been. I was
stricken. How could he tell so easily? Other than telling my
mother and my priest so very little, I had never let a word slip
to anyone.

He continued to surprise me by offering me free
counseling. I was a photography student at the time at the

local community college, and his home office wasn't too far from there. I could go to see him twice a week after class.

I was twenty-six years old the first time I received counseling for my childhood abuse. I weighed 160 at the time, and found myself uncomfortable, even fearful about being attractive again. I had such high hopes this would be the help I needed to feel stable and happy and to be a good wife.

The first appointment I had with him started with a leisurely tour of his home, including his and his wife's bedroom (she was never home when I had appointments with him). This was my first red flag.

For a young woman going to a very conservative church, his methods seemed off kilter. They made me uncomfortable at times, and I even wondered if it was sinful to listen to him. He spoke often about my auras, for example—a concept not exactly condoned by my church.

He asked me probing questions about my relationship with Tom. I was ashamed to say how hateful I was toward Tom. He said it was only natural, considering my past.

Gradually, over the course of six sessions, I saw where his idea of counseling was leading. His implication was that all I needed was a positive sexual experience to get over my aversion to sex with my husband. By then it was obvious where he intended the positive sexual experience to come from. Sorry I had ever trusted him, I left and never went back.

I couldn't so easily turn my back on the effects of all of his probing questions though. I had kept all of the abuse, and the feelings it raised, under a tightly closed lid for so long. This episode took the lid off. It felt like I was a can of worms. The top had been pried off, and now the worms were loose and crawling all over me. There was no way I was ever going to get them back in the can.

I was desperate now, and feeling suicidal. I told Tom I needed a Christian counselor *now*, and it needed to be a woman.

He found a wonderful young Christian woman named Paula. I was one of her first patients; in fact, she had to tape our sessions and allow someone to review them and advise her. There was a drawback to my liking her so much though. While I trusted her and could have made major progress, I didn't want to say anything that would cause her to dislike me. As a result, I kept most of my deepest beliefs hidden within.

One thing she insisted I do, however, was tell Tom I had been molested by my father. This was the one place I did not want to go. She gave me homework after every session, and I dutifully did them all. This, though, I just could not do.

Imagining his anger, I trembled at the thought. After all, I had painted myself as a good, pure Catholic girl. I'd made him wait until we were married for sex. Now I was supposed to reveal to him that I was dirty and used? He already knew I was broken; now he would know why. I just couldn't tell him. He would leave me for sure, or so I thought.

Finally, she insisted I bring him to a counseling session and tell him in her presence. She said she would help him understand. As it happened, she didn't need to.

With a trembling voice and much sobbing, at times almost impossible to understand, I told him. Eyes downcast, I awaited his response.

This blessed man came and knelt before me with tears in his own eyes, and put his head in my lap. Instead of the words of condemnation I expected, he said, "I'm so relieved! All this time I thought it was me."

He thought I had found him repulsive. He thought I didn't love him. Now he knew the truth, and it set *him* free. His love has never wavered. He's been my rock all these years. I thank God every day for his faithfulness and patience.

My daughter, Jaynie, once asked him, if he could have seen into the future and seen all of the things I'd put him through, all of the drama and expense, would he still have married me?

Without a pause, he said, "Yes! I loved her that much." And he still does.

Chapter 12: Lies and Consequences

A truthful witness saves lives, but a deceitful witness
speaks lies [and endangers lives] (Proverbs 14:25).

There were other lies I came to regret telling. One very important untruth was when Tom and I had been married for over two years. We'd had sex at least six times, and I couldn't understand why I wasn't pregnant yet. (Go figure.) I wanted a baby to love. This was the one honest part of the whole situation, and the main reason I had gone through with getting married. My sister already had a baby boy. I loved him so much I sometimes wondered if I would be able to love my own with an equal intensity.

I found an obstetrical practice to see if they could tell me why I hadn't conceived yet. They gave me a chart where I was to keep track of my menstrual cycle and our times of intercourse. Intercourse was to be marked with an X. I did this, but on my way to the following appointment, I glanced down at the chart on the passenger's seat and I saw its lonely X. At stop lights, I randomly added more Xs to make it look like I was really trying. All those extra Xs were my lie. This went on for months.

Despite the incredible odds, I conceived on our third anniversary, July 14, 1975. As it happened, it was the *only* time we'd had sex the entire summer. We'd had a house guest for two months. Since her bedroom was next to ours, I used the excuse that I was afraid she would hear us to avoid sex. Even though we were officially "trying," Tom reluctantly agreed.

I went to the doctors in September, when I was eight weeks pregnant. After examining me, he decided I wasn't that far along. Because I couldn't admit to all those fake Xs, I didn't correct him when he wrote down I was only four weeks pregnant. I wanted to say I was either eight weeks pregnant or not at all. But I didn't want to tell him why. *Oh, well*, I thought, *the baby will come when it's ready*. If I'd only known.

Ultrasounds are considered routine today to verify due dates and fetal health in pregnancy, but they weren't available in the 1970s. When I was four months along, by my knowledge (three in my doctor's), the baby kicked hard when the doctor was listening to my belly. He mumbled to himself, and charted the baby just might be four months after all. However, my ninth month came along, and my cervix hadn't even started to thin as expected. Then he smugly said his original estimation had been correct, and let me go for another four weeks. When I still didn't go into labor, he waited two weeks more. This made me ten and a half months pregnant—six weeks overdue! In my mind, I was completely to blame, as none of this would've happened had I just been able to be truthful about all those fake Xs.

In retrospect, the facts are quite different, and the blame was not entirely mine. I'd told my doctors I was leaking fluid those last six weeks. They said it was probably just urine. I'd also told them for the last two weeks that the baby had stopped moving except for getting the hiccups. They were unconcerned.

92

Roxanne Fawley

I *finally* went into labor at ten and a half months. I was so happy the morning I started labor! The waiting was over, I thought. Little did I know the truth. It was just beginning. After laboring for over twenty-four hours, I still hadn't dilated past four centimeters. That's when they started me on Pitocin, a drug to make the contractions harder (as if they weren't hard enough!). Still no change in the cervix. Then they decided to break my water to get things rolling. Only trouble was, there wasn't any left! I can still recall the look on the doctors' face when he realized it was going to be a difficult, dry birth.

Thirty-two hours had gone by and I still hadn't dilated. The baby began to show signs of stress, so finally they decided it was necessary to do an emergency C-section.

My baby was in distress, and it was all because of my lie.

They were in such a hurry to get the baby out of me that they ripped apart the last few layers of tissue in order to lessen the risk of cutting into him. Yes, him! At last, they delivered my son, Thomas "Casey" Fawley. He was a ten-pound, dehydrated, peeling, wrinkled, and bald baby! His head was fifteen centimeters; it had never even been able to enter the birth canal.

He'd also had three bowel movements, called meconium while still in the womb. This is a very dangerous condition, but because he was so large, and with the lack of amniotic fluid, he hadn't breathed any of it into his lungs. The meconium had stayed in his bottom area, thus saving his life. The first blessing of the whole experience.

He was a healthy, beautiful, big, baby boy. The first time I nursed him, the nurse said, "He took six ounces! From the breast!" By the time we took him home seven days later, he weighed twelve pounds. I was admonished to not lift anything over five pounds. Yeah right, like my twelve-pound baby was going to lift himself?

There was another blessing and her name was Leslie. She was one of the nurses who cared for me during my labor, the only one who stayed with me during the entire time. Even after her shift was over, she stayed and comforted me the best she could. The other nurses were unsympathetic to my pain and indifferent to my plight. In fact, it seemed their job was to make me more miserable.

Even colder, my doctor told Tom and me none of these problems would've happened if I hadn't gained so much weight! The truth was, by my fourth month I had gained only five pounds. It was at that appointment during the examination that one of the doctors from the practice tried to express milk from my breasts by massaging them. I only weighed 145 pounds at that visit. I felt as if I'd been molested. Now I know that indeed I was, as no other woman I've asked has ever had such a thing happen to her in her fourth month. Indeed, no other woman has told me they've had an OB doctor *massage* their breasts *ever*, to express milk or otherwise.

By now the reader should know me well enough to understand that I felt as if I were to blame for that doctor's actions, and proceeded to gain weight at a rapid pace. I had gained sixty pounds by my due date, and twenty more by the time I delivered. I wasn't molested again though. In fact, one of the other doctors in the practice, who saw me toward the end of my pregnancy, said I was disgusting. He told me if I'd been his wife, he wouldn't have even been able to touch me. He said I looked more like a cow than a woman.

Success. So why did I cry all the way home?

Roxanne Fawley

By the time Casey was six months old, I had lost sixty of the pounds I'd gained. I'd told Tom if we wanted another child in the next three years we'd better start trying then. He, of course, was game. I conceived on our first try—Valentine's Day, 1977.

This time we went to a different group of doctors and hospital. At the first visit, I told the doctor that because I wasn't going to get fat this time, I would like to have this baby naturally. He looked at me oddly and asked, "Don't you know why you had to have a C-section?"

I said, "Yes. I gained too much weight." Then I proceeded to tell him that I worked at a health spa now, and even taught aerobics, so it was most assuredly *not* going to happen again.

What he said next shocked both Tom and me. He explained my gaining weight had nothing to do with my C-section. The reason I had not dilated was because my cervix had scar tissue from having been cauterized. Since scar tissue can't stretch, I had been unable to dilate. It was all in my chart from the previous doctors. They had written the truth in the chart and told us a lie. Even though we were taken aback to hear the truth, I still felt to blame, because of *my* lie—all those fake Xs on that chart.

Chapter 13: Making Progress

*He who deals wisely and heeds [God's] Word and
counsel shall find good, and whoever leans on, trusts
in, and is confident in the Lord—happy, blessed, and
fortunate is he (Proverbs 16:20).*

Years later, I lied again. This time to a remarkable man
who was counseling me. Dr. Flachier was a wonderful,
capable psychologist and a wise, kind man. I'd been counseled
by others, many times before. It always led to me becoming
even more depressed and suicidal, because I would literally
rather die than say out loud what I believed to be the truth
about my problems—the lie that I had asked for and enjoyed
the sexual abuse.

I never believed what I actually went through warranted
the extent of the depression I was in or the problems I was
having. I never believed I even deserved to *be* counseled.
What I did believe was I was evil and deserved to be punished
or destroyed. So what did I do? I lied again.

This is very hard to admit and write about. I wrote Dr.
Flachier a long letter about horrible things my father did to
me. Although some were true, most were lies. I wrote about
terrible incidents I thought would lend credence to and explain
my messed up way of thinking.

One of the lies was about how my father and grandfather
had brutally raped me. The truth was, they had only used

their fingers. I told about being passed around to my father's friends and other terrible untruths. They backfired, like all lies do. Dr. Flachier, of course, believed every sordid word and tried to counsel and comfort me. I, of course, couldn't accept any of it, because so much of it was lies. So much for thinking a violent rape or two would explain a destructive thought process like mine. Surely it could *never* be rationalized by the pitiful excuse that was my unspeakable belief: I had *liked* it.

By this time though, I was a Christian. I didn't have complete assurance of my salvation, but I did have a 98 percent working conscience, and it told me I had to tell Dr. Flachier the unbearable fact—that most of what I had shared in that letter was not true. It wouldn't however, let me share my real belief, the one causing all my grief.

Though I fully expected him to be disgusted with me, even hate me and never believe another word I said, I had to tell him it was lies, and try to explain why I'd done such a terrible thing. So through my tears, I told him I thought what had actually happened to me was not bad enough. As a result, I made up the worse abuse. Because I still could not admit I had sometimes sought my father's sexual attention and received pleasure by it, I called them all lies. (I know now, in truth, I did fear my father. I did cry many times. I often felt shame and blame and wanted it to stop.)

Dr. Flachier did not throw up his hands in disgust or order me out of his office as I had feared. He did not even refuse to see me anymore. I wasn't the first patient to have lied to him for similar reasons. He told me it took a lot of courage to tell him about the lies. Too bad I still didn't have the guts to tell him what I thought was the truth; I thought I had enjoyed it, and the only way I believed it would stop was if one of us was to die. This was why I tried to end my life when I

98

was fourteen, and so many times after. It was also why, even though my father was now dead, I was still suicidal well into my 50s.

Dr. Flachier was the one who wisely recommended I attend DBT. He noticed how I kept discounting most of his help and counseling, even though he didn't know it was because of my innate belief that I was evil, not merely sick. He had the insight to realize in a group setting I might see my problem in someone else and be able to see the truth about myself.

That's exactly what happened. I had all this compassion for everyone in the group, but none for myself, and they pointed this out to me. Being in group therapy, I slowly began to allow myself the same grace and help that I so willingly offered to others.

Chapter 14: Dr. Bell

The wise also will hear and increase in learning, and the person of understanding will acquire skill and attain to sound counsel [so that he may be able to steer his course rightly] (Proverbs 1:5).

Another man who played an indispensable role in my recovery was Dr. Verle Bell. He was my psychiatrist during one of my hospitalizations in a Grand Rapids institution for mental health. I had stayed in this hospital numerous times, but I bless the day God gave *him* to be my doctor.

He shared with me the fact that he ran a Bible study every week, and invited Tom and me to come and see what it was all about. He counseled a group of us with godly principles. This was completely voluntary on his part. His true passion was counseling, but he believed there was a greater need for Christian psychiatrists, thus making that his profession. He taught us truths he had gleaned from the Bible, such as— you may feel worthless, but you can no longer *be* worthless, because the price Christ paid for you with His life made you precious.

Another prodigious lesson I learned from him was, even if I never did another good thing for the rest of my life, God would not love me any less; and if I did do only good things from now on, He couldn't love me any more than he did right then. My heavenly Father's love is not based on my actions, but on Jesus'! He loves me for Jesus' sake!

In time (and I mean over a period of years) Dr. Bell was able to make me see I possessed a sick kind of pride to believe I alone, out of all the sinners in the world, was too evil for God's grace to cover me. How could God's grace cover me, I wondered? I who had liked the sexual abuse? Wasn't His grace just for true victims, the ones like my cousin who had hated it and cried?

Then Dr. Bell graciously gave me an example that would change my life, using his own three daughters. I knew them all very well from our weekly Bible studies. He said, if he had tried anything sexual with his oldest daughter, she would've had him in jail before the day's end. Any attempts with his second daughter would have resulted in her plotting his death while he slept. But his third daughter, who I *knew* was the sweetest and most loving of the three, would have welcomed him.

He then asked, "Do you believe she is my most evil daughter?"

For the first time I caught a glimpse of myself as a dear, sweet *little* girl. I found myself overwhelmed with the intense feelings of the hurt and pain of a victim. But the truth of it all allowed me to finally start receiving the help I so desperately needed. I had taken an enormous step. Now I needed to take an even greater step—one of becoming a survivor.

In the DBT group setting, whenever I would begin to judge myself harshly, they would ask me if I would judge any of them this way for the same exact thing. The answer was always "no."

Roxanne Fawley

They told me to try to say to myself the things I always said to them—kind, wise, and loving things. Truths. I slowly began to catch myself and ease up from the devastating judgmentalism I used on myself, and instead, started loving myself and giving myself grace.

Grace! "Grace, grace, God's grace! Grace that is greater than all my sin!" So goes an old hymn.[1]

Dr. Bell said to me, "So, let's say Roxanne needs a bazillion, quadrillion buckets of grace, when everyone else only needs one bucket. A bazillion, quadrillion from infinity is still infinity!" Since God's grace was infinite, it was sufficient for me! And I do believe I had sinned as well as been sinned against.

I once heard a sermon entitled, "Depression: Is It a Sin?" The gist of it was that even though depression in and of itself was not a sin, nursing it was. And boy, could I nurse my depression! I'm now able to see some of the "whys" and don't take *all* the blame onto myself. I have confessed my part and have been forgiven. But—and this is a huge *but*—I should've been able to dance around naked and not have a father who got turned on. My own three daughters have such a loving and pure father. They could have wiggled naked in his lap and he would be incapable of arousal. This is what every child deserves.

I am so grateful for Tom. God gave me, as Joyce Meyer puts it, "double for my trouble," in him. Sure, I had an abusive father for eighteen years, but I've had Tom for most of my years and the rest of my life! We've already shared forty-two years, and God willing, we'll share many more.

---

1. Julia H. Johnston, "Grace Greater Than Our Sin," copyright 1911. Public Domain.

But I Liked It...and Other Lies

In Isaiah 61:7, God says, "Instead of your [former] shame you shall have a twofold recompense; instead of dishonor and reproach [your people] (That's me!) shall rejoice in their portion. Therefore in their land they shall possess double [what they had forfeited]; everlasting joy shall be theirs." Isn't God wonderful?

I'm now sixty, and for the last six years I have been emotionally, mentally, and spiritually stable. I'm still obese, but well on my way to losing the safety fat. Tom and I wake up early and do devotions, and on most mornings go for a walk. I also use the gym five days a week. I'm in the best physical health I've been in for years. At this writing, I'm seventy pounds lighter than my heaviest weight!

I'm still on medication and always will be for my bipolar disorder, but I haven't needed any further counseling since my days at InterAct of Michigan.

My whole previous life was one of fear. My father seemed to take pleasure in hurting us. I have seen my mother socked in the face to the point of having her teeth knocked out. I have seen her pushed down and shoved into walls. I heard him say terrible, vile things to her. I remember her lying on the chairs under the tablecloth of the dining room table, hiding, just to get away from his drunken advances.

I saw and heard all my brothers' and sisters' physical and mental abuse.

Once, when my brother Marty got older and strong enough, I watched him beat his own father to a pulp. He was just protecting my mother, but couldn't stop punching him until he'd broken our father's dentures and thrown him off the back porch. This beating resulted in my father's having the two broken arms Tom saw when he first met him. How awful

104

for a son to have to beat his father! I can still see my father lying on the ground, helpless and bloody. It was my job to hose all the blood off him and help get him ready to go to the doctor. We feared him a lot less after this, but the damage to all our psyches had been done.

I remember my sister getting mocked by my father on her fourteenth birthday in January. "Happy birthday, fat ass," was what he said to her. Can you imagine? She ran upstairs to her bedroom in tears. She wouldn't even eat a piece of her own birthday cake. She lost twenty pounds by summer.

My younger brother Kevin was born on our dad's birthday and was considered the favorite son. He experienced his share of abuse and witnessed ours. We were all scarred in different ways.

A house of fear is not of God. He does not give us a spirit of fear but of power, and of love and a sound mind (see 2 Timothy 1:7). Also, there is no fear in love; but perfect love casts out fear, because fear has torment (see 1 John 4:18).

Ours was not a house of love. When I was ten, I was given a spirit board for my birthday. It was thought to be just a game. But it opened up another kind of darkness to my siblings and me as we "played" with it.

I also dabbled in daily horoscopes and séances at sleepovers. I believe these things all give Satan a foothold in our lives.

Liquor is also called "spirits" for a reason. I believe that when my father fed his flesh with alcohol, it made him want to feed it sexually too. This might explain why he would almost ignore me when he was sober, which was usually just a short time when he was first home from school. Being a teacher meant he had every evening, weekend, and holiday to get drunk. He had all summer to imbibe. He was drunk more than not.

But I Liked It...and Other Lies

From my earliest memories, I suffered from terrible nightmares. I'd feel terror and have demonic dreams. I remember one night at the age of four I dreamt I was looking up at a circle of angels. Then I looked down at a beautiful cake. It then turned into a squirming, rotting mass of worms. When I looked up again, it was demons looking down at me. I remember wondering, if I lived to be twenty-one, if I'd still be having dreams like these. Well, I did. I even had weird out-of-body experiences where I would wake up, but not be able to move. This continued into my adulthood until Karel invited Tom and me to a seminar that talked about such things. It was there I learned I needed to confess and repent of my involvement with these former practices. I confessed and asked to be forgiven and cleansed of their effect, and I was! I have been completely free from those awful dreams ever since.

I did, however, suffer from PTSD (post-traumatic stress disorder). I was plagued with flashbacks, and memories would surface which would make me feel evil and depressed.

After I graduated from DBT, I signed up for the PTSD counseling. It was an amazing part of my recovery. I had two counselors during the ten weeks it took to complete the course. The first therapist left to have a baby. It was all part of God's plan. The second counselor didn't know me quite as well and I needed her perspective to get through to the end. When it was over, I was able to talk about any part of my abuse without breaking down. It was horrendously difficult to go through, but I wouldn't be writing this story or talking about it had I not stuck it out to the end.

Chapter 15: Extremes

To everything there is a season, and a time for every matter or purpose under heaven...a time to break down and a time to build up...A time to weep and a time to laugh (Ecclesiastes 31, 3, 4).

When I was thirty-seven and our nineteenth anniversary was approaching, I decided I wanted to have another baby. I was feeling pretty good, even though I weighed about 260 pounds. I don't think Tom thought it would really happen, so he agreed to try. Surprise, surprise! I got pregnant with our fourth child on our nineteenth anniversary. We just knew it would be a boy, so we didn't even pick out a girl's name. The baby was due on my brother and father's birthday so we decided we would give him my brother's name and call him Kevin Thomas, though we planned to call him Tommy. I had always wanted a Tommy and even though I already had Thomas "Casey," everyone had always called him Casey from the beginning. So this time I was going to get my Tommy. This was before the days of ultrasounds to determine the sex of the child.

Even though I wanted this baby and tried for it, I was still embarrassed to be pregnant at my age with my medical background. Here I was—bipolar, overweight and I'd already had the prescribed three C-sections. As a result, I waited four months before going to see my doctors.

But I Liked It...and Other Lies

It was a good thing I went then, though, because as it turned out, I had gestational diabetes. I had to prick my finger four times a day, take insulin twice a day, and go on a strict diet. I actually lost ten pounds during the pregnancy.

I continued taking my medications for stabilizing my mood swings, just like I had with my other three pregnancies.

The day of the birth arrived and I was so excited! We went to the hospital in the morning. The plan was for me to be awake during this birth. I had been under general anesthesia for my other three, and I was thrilled to be "present."

They tried to give me a spinal. "Roll into a ball," they said, and injected a needle into my spine. Wow, did it hurt! But it didn't work. They tried a second time. They still couldn't hit the right spot. They said they would try one more time, but if it didn't work, they would have to give me general anesthesia. When they put the needle in for the third time, it actually broke off in me! No more trying, they said. Something in my mother's heart made me beg.

"Please, this is my last chance to see my own child's birth," I cried.

They relented. "This is the last time though," they said. I prayed, "Please God, let it work!" It did! Everyone cheered. Little did we know, the baby's very life was at stake.

Everything following this happened fast. They performed the C-section and I saw my baby born. They quickly whisked it past me and I saw it was green! *So babies are actually born green*, I thought. It wasn't the bloody red that Hollywood always showed. Then I heard someone say, "It's a girl! What's her name?"

Roxanne Fawley

I was so surprised it was a girl, I just blurted out, "Mia Kathleen."

You see, when I was expecting our first child, I wanted to name it Mia if it was a girl. Mia means "beloved daughter of mine." Then Tom had a dream where he kept saying, "Mia is a bean!" As a result, whenever people asked me what I would name a girl if I had one, and I said," Mia," Tom, if he was around, would always say, "Is a bean, is a bean." Something I didn't want to hear for the rest of her life, so I changed my girl's name choice to Suzanne.

Little did we know, Tom was actually being prophetic. Mia was a bean. A little green bean! Everyone laughed.

It was no laughing matter though. Her green coating was meconium and she had breathed some of it into her lungs, giving her aspiration pneumonia. Had I been given the general anesthesia, she would've been under its influence also, and she wouldn't have had the strength she needed to breathe. Getting that last spinal helped to save her life. She had a terrible time trying to breathe.

Tom and the kids were given a chance to hold her, but I wasn't. They sewed me up and then asked me if I wanted to see my baby before I went up to my room. I, of course, said, "Yes."

They wheeled me into a room full of babies in incubators. There was one baby who was hooked up to a bunch of wires and monitors. Its chest was rising and falling 100 miles an hour. They merely said, "There's your baby."

I asked, "Is she going to die?"

They answered my question with the sad news that they didn't know.

109

But I Liked It...and Other Lies

As I was taken to my room, Mia was taken to another hospital that had a neonatal intensive care unit.

I was so worried. Here I was in one hospital while my baby was in another. It had all taken place on Monday, April 30, 1990. Just two days later, while my sister Kathy was visiting, some people came into my room and asked me if I'd like to get Mia baptized. What I *heard,* though, was "Your baby is about to die!" With my sister's help, I left the hospital against medical advice. We rushed to the other hospital so I could see Mia before she died.

The church we were attending had a prayer chain going for her, and my father-in-law had never left her side. When we got there, I was greeted with wonderful news. Mia was getting better, not worse! The nurses were calling her "Miracle Mia." It was one of the happiest days of my life!

Unfortunately, the doctor in charge wouldn't let me nurse her unless I went off all my medication for at least two weeks. This was the length of time it took for the medicine to get out of one's system to a safe extent. I had nursed my other three children safely while still on medication, but he wouldn't even consider it.

My best friend, Susie Meschke, who was a nurse, was able to get an electric breast pump for me. I began the pump and dump process. I did just fine for about six weeks. In fact I was super mom! I was cooking, cleaning, shopping, nursing, and loving it all. You might even say I was euphoric. That is the manic side of a bipolar disorder, depression being the other.

I started to not need sleep. I had oodles of energy. I was having a severe manic episode. Inevitably, I began to have unwanted thoughts, like—I had too many things. More than I deserved. I thought Mia had too much also. *We don't deserve to be this happy and blessed*, was just one of the irrational thoughts I had.

Soon after, I began to slip into a deep postpartum depression. I started having suicidal ideations for myself *and* Mia. Thoughts like: *I can't take my life and leave Tom stuck caring for a new baby. I'll have to take her with me when I die.*

Thoughts like these and worse scared me so much that I told Tom a few of the ones I was having. He, of course, immediately had me hospitalized.

Mia was cared for by my sister-in-law, Emmy, for about a week. Later, she went to stay with a friend of ours, the DeVissers, who lived way out in Plainwell, Michigan. Because they were so far away, it was hard for Tom to visit her. Also, Tom's parents weren't comfortable going to a stranger's house to visit her, so they decided *they* would take care of her. My mother-in-law had a full-time job, but dad was retired and he took over her total care, and loved every minute of it.

While I was in the hospital, they had to bind my breasts to stop the milk flow. I was so determined to die I ended up in a padded cell so I couldn't harm myself. It was during that hospital stay in the mental ward I was given my first ECT treatments. I was thirty-eight years old. After that it gets hazy, because ECT has the side effect of short-term memory loss. So this next part is pretty much what people have told me.

Even though I was out of the hospital after two weeks, I was still unable to care properly for Mia. I'm told I was distant and unfeeling toward her. I wasn't trusted to care for her until late September. Even then, Dad Fawley came over every day. He was a wonderful man. The father I'd always wanted.

I would go through all the motions of taking care of her, but my heart was just not in it.

I did take many pictures and videos of her though. Now I love to look at them, and try to enjoy the adorable baby I can see she was.

What I do remember is the day when Mia was about three years old, and I discovered what a precious gift she was. It's like I woke up and found I had this sweet, enjoyable little girl for the first time. I've enjoyed her ever since. (Although the teen years were a bit rough!) She is now a talented sweetheart, complete with the heart needed for the work she does—caring for the disabled and elderly.

Prior to DBT, I used to believe another diabolical lie. I thought that just because I'd been abused, I was destined to *be* an abuser. The fear I could abuse my children added fuel to my suicidal thinking. I would die before I would do anything like sexually abuse one of my children. I'd sometimes have nightmares where I was being sexual with my children. I was so afraid; if I could do it in my dreams, I was capable of being a monster, period! Also, everything I'd ever read or heard on the subject of sexual abuse said the abuser had always been abused themselves. I thought it was a given. This made me want to die before anything even close to this could happen. I had a hard time changing my children's diapers, and I would often have Tom bathe them because I was afraid to touch them in the wrong way.

After one of my suicide attempts, I finally shared this fear, and was told that 85 percent of abused children do *not* go on to become abusers themselves. My personal research brought a welcome confirmation that most abuse survivors do not go on to become molesters themselves. God showed me I was in the 85 percent; thank goodness, dreams are not facts.

Unfortunately, before I learned this, I tried to end my life by taking all my prescription drugs. I ended up in intensive care with a tube down my throat. I got chemical pneumonia from inhaling the charcoal they had pumped into my stomach to absorb the medicine.

I remember waking up in intensive care, having charcoal all over my face and in my hair. I couldn't talk, because of the tube that was helping me breathe. My arms and legs were tied to the bed. They were afraid I might try to pull the tube out since I was suicidal. Tom was only allowed to see me once a day for fifteen minutes at a time.

After many hours had passed in which I felt alone and frightened, I started to not be able to breathe. I looked to the nurses standing around their station. Since I couldn't tell them what was happening to me, I started banging my wedding ring against the metal bed railing. The nurses just looked at me and then went back to whatever they were doing. I began to bang both my ring fingers against the bed rails. They gave me no response at all this time. Everything began to get dark. The last thing I heard was the breathing machine's alarm going off. It was alerting them to the fact my tube was plugged with mucus and I wasn't getting any air. I came to with them all around me, suctioning the airway. I wanted to tell them that was why I was banging my rings on the railings, but I didn't really blame them for ignoring the crazy person who was there because she tried to take her own life. *I obviously didn't care so why should they?* I thought to myself.

I remember after this attempt that the doctor on duty became so angry at me! He seemed furious that I didn't even have a residual effect from the massive overdose. He shouted, "At the very least, your liver should be damaged!"

I think he might have been trying to use reverse psychology on me, to try and get me to defend myself. But I just agreed with him. I *didn't* deserve to be alive and healthy with no adverse aftereffects.

Chapter 16: Deliver Me

You are a hiding place for me; You, Lord, preserve me from trouble, You surround me with songs and shouts of deliverance (Psalms 32:7).

And in the night His song shall be with me, a prayer to the God of my life (Psalms 42:8).

Another vicious cycle cruelly plagued me. It included the thought, *If only Tom would just die.* This would come unbidden and torture me. I'd think: *I wouldn't have to worry about having sex.*

Sex always led to me mentally returning to the scene of my crime—being with my father.

Becoming appalled at myself for thinking such thoughts toward Tom, I chastised myself. Deadly reasonings would flood my mind, thoughts like: *If anyone needs to die, it's me. The kids need their dad more than they need me. He's their provider and real caregiver.*

I couldn't divorce him. He was such a good man no one would understand. Once again, I would conclude the only solution to everything was, *I'm the one who needs to die!* It would be a just punishment for me for thinking such horrible thoughts toward such a wonderful man. Thus the vicious cycle would go around and around until I longed for death and the peace I thought it would bring.

But I Liked It...and Other Lies

In the event I would be able to successfully take my own life, I believed I would go to be with Jesus, so even the fear of hell wasn't a deterrent. But I did *not* want to leave my children with such a horrible legacy. Suicide. I, of all people, knew the self-blaming thoughts that would follow a death like that.

Nevertheless, one night, or rather early morning, around 4:00 a.m., I was being sorely tempted to end my life. It had been a while since I had been intimate with Tom and the pressure (all of my own making) was detrimentally intense. I was in anguish of mind and spirit, feeling hopeless. I did not want to be with Tom and all it would entail, but I hated to deprive him of what I thought he wanted. *Maybe if I died, he would finally get the wife he deserved,* I thought. I was in despair. In keeping with my usual MO, I was fast convincing myself that the only way out of this pain was death. I began to believe the lie that my family would be better off, and I would actually be doing them a favor, if I would just be done with it and die. A lie straight from the pit of hell.

I was flipping through the TV channels trying to postpone what I knew I was going to do. Overdose. Again. Maybe this time I would be successful. *Please, God,* I silently prayed, *let me come home to You!* All of a sudden, a singer I had never even heard of before came on a station I don't remember. A Christian artist named Margaret Becker. She began to sing a song that became my prayer that night: "Deliver Me." The words went like this:

> I was just about to tell You.
> What I'm sure You already know.
> How my heart is tight with crying.
> In my soul is Arctic blue.
> 'Cause I've seen some tears that didn't move me,
> Whispered words I didn't mean

116

Roxanne Fawley

Held back all my love for anger.
Grown so weak in all these things,
So in all these things;
Deliver me from me, and to deliver me to You.
Come and set me free, come and find me, tried and true.
Come on now, deliver me from me!
I was just about to run away.
As far as far could go.
When I recognized my cruelest captors.
Living right inside my soul.
And I can't escape their endless movements
Cannot shed them like a skin.
Can't control all these emotions.
Cannot live while they're within.
So in all these things,
Deliver me from me and deliver me to You.
Come and set me free. Come and find me, tried and true.
Come on now, come on now, now.
Deliver me from me.
And now I'm falling, falling.
Cause there's nowhere else that I can go.
Dreaming of Your arms of mercy.
They are soft as the new winter's snow. Deliver me from me.[2]

Her song was used by God to save my life that early morning. I prayed with all my heart these words and was spared from the evil promptings of my flesh and Satan.

2. Margaret Becker and Robbie Nevil, *Deliver Me*, from *Falling Forward*, Sparrow Records, 1998.

Chapter 17: Finally Whole

A bruised reed He will not break, and a smoldering (dimly burning) wick He will not quench, till He brings justice and a just cause to victory (Matthew 12:20).

Even after all my mental and emotional healing, sex continued to be physically painful. Penetration hurt and so would urination afterward. I couldn't help but wonder if there might *still* be something wrong with me physically. I went to see another doctor, this time an urologist. After examining me, he recommended I get vaginal physical therapy! I didn't even know such a thing existed. How awkward and embarrassing would it be? Then I thought of how far I'd come. How difficult it had been for me to bare my soul in counseling and DBT. Was I really going to let a little discomfort come between me and a really intimate life with Tom? I went, but not without trepidation.

The female therapist was very professional and understanding. She said I was wise and courageous. And since I had already spent so much time, effort, and money on my emotional healing, it only made sense to invest in, and submit to, physical therapy as well.

The medical term for painful intercourse is dyspareunia. My therapist told me that when sex hurts it's most likely more than just a physical issue. Painful intercourse causes a vicious cycle of its own. Sex hurts so you tense up. This causes more

119

pain, which leads to less frequent intercourse, which then leads to more tenseness, more pain, and on and on.

The good news? After only five treatments, I learned to relax to the point of no more painful intercourse. I'm thrilled to be able to say I am pain free, emotionally and physically for the first time in my life.

Our marriage is now wonderful in every way. I used to have to get drunk or high in order to have sex. But God's Word says in Ephesians 5:18-20, "And do not get drunk with wine, for that is debauchery; but ever be filled and stimulated with the [Holy] Spirit. Speak out one to another in psalms and hymns and spiritual songs, offering praise with voices [and instruments] and making melody with all your heart to the Lord. At all times and for everything giving thanks in the name of our Lord Jesus Christ to God the Father."

I need to be filled with God's Spirit in order to be intimate with Tom and not go back to the abuse in my mind. For me it helps when we're together to turn on Christian music. It's a beautiful backdrop for making love. Now, by the grace of God, I'm able to love my husband with my whole self. It's the way God always intended it to be.

It's been a long, rough road, but at last I am able to *enjoy* Tom *and* our lovemaking. God is so powerful and good. He has been with me through everything.

Recently, my daughter Jaynie wrote that a story she'd posted on a social media site had been plagiarized. Her story was about something a friend had told her. It went something like this:

A girl had been sexually abused by her father and she was having trouble with bitterness. She asked her youth pastor to pray for her. He prayed, and while he prayed, God told him He wanted her to ask Him where *He* had been during the abuse. She was crying so hard, she couldn't speak so her pastor asked Him for her. Jesus told him to tell her that He was in the bathroom. When she heard that, her eyes got really big. She sobbed—that's where she would go to hide and cry.

I posted that the story gave me goose bumps and made me cry. Then Jaynie posted me back with, "Have you ever asked God where He was while you were being molested?"

I told her I hadn't. She told me to ask Him right then.

I became quiet within myself and started thinking of all the places the abuse had happened. I figured when I asked, He'd probably say those places. He didn't. He distinctly told me He was *in* me every time, the whole time. He Himself was also abused by my father and grandfather.

I posted this answer on the Internet and my daughter Jaynie wrote back, "Oh, dear Jesus! I'm crying. Of course He was!"

I answered back I was overcome with the knowledge that He had felt everything I had, and I'd never realized it before.

Then my oldest daughter, Suzy, posted, "God brought something good—even out of Jaynie's being plagiarized."

Jaynie wrote back, "He breaks every chain! He died for you and He was abused for you. He didn't prevent what happened, but He chose to take the abuse with you. For some, His presence is enough. For you He needed to be able to tell you someday (today), 'Roxanne, I couldn't just watch. I had to participate.' That is amazing! And if God was abused with you, He is being abused every day in the lives of all the child sex slaves being trafficked around the world. Not because He has to, but because He wants to. Because He desires that those kids be free someday, and He will be able to say to them, 'That happened to Me too.' And He'll be able to break the chains of addiction, guilt, oppression, blame, worthlessness, dirtiness and shame." I say, praise His holy name!

Epilogue

M any times I felt prompted by God to write my story, but I always had excuses why I shouldn't. The main one always being that it wouldn't have a happy ending because I still struggled with depression and intimacy issues.

I don't have those excuses anymore thanks to God, the good men and women He used to bless me, and the DBT and PTSD therapy I received at InterAct of Michigan in Kalamazoo, Michigan.

I have become emotionally stable and even intimately close to my husband. My children have also noticed a tremendous difference in me. For the first time in their lives, they can love me without the constant fear of losing me.

When the promptings to write became more frequent, I still continued to procrastinate, even though everyone I dared to share my story with would say, "You really should write a book."

I told myself, or rather listened when the enemy said, "Who could possibly be helped by you? Who do you think you are? Why go through the pain and trouble for nothing? Who would you get to publish it? You can't write. Who wants to read another book about abuse?"

Believing these lies, I put off writing and ignored God's nudges until one day when I was watching Joyce Meyer on TV. She was telling us about the death of her younger brother—how all he had left behind was an eight by ten manila envelope with only four things inside it. Then she asked, "What would be your legacy if you died?" *Stamping stuff,* I thought, because that's my hobby and I have a whole room devoted to it. *Who would want that?* Then I thought about my other hobby—photography and all the things I'd collected over the years pertaining to it. I was thinking, *One of the kids might like them,* when all of a sudden I heard the Holy Spirit whisper in my heart, "Your story." All my excuses came flooding in and drowned Him out.

I stood up from my chair and went into the computer room. I checked my e-mail and there was a devotional from a computer ministry I subscribed to. I started reading it. It was about a woman who had been prompted by God to write a book years earlier, and how she had ignored Him. Later, she found a book about the very subject she wanted to write about, even to the point of including some of the same Scriptures she was going to use. She concluded that God wanted the message told, and because she wouldn't obey and write it, He gave it to someone who would! Then the devotional asked, "Is there something the Lord has been prompting you to do? Why not pray about it now and make a start to obey Him."

Right then I prayed and felt God telling me to just start writing. I said, "Okay, I'll write two sentences if You'll help me."

I began writing longhand, and thirty pages later, stopped. He'd given me the title and the beginnings of the first four chapters. I began writing every day for two or more hours until I had the first rough draft. Very rough, I might add.

Roxanne Fawley

I let my sister and a few friends read it. They all said it was a good start and had an important message that needed to be heard. I wondered if any publisher would think so. Rough as it was, I sent it to a Christian publisher, and they believed it *was* worth finishing. I got a very low grade for grammar though, just a three out of ten! I knew I would need skilled help. I found some in friends, Midgie Bardo, Anna Stryd, and my sister, Kathy Paul. I am so thankful for their assistance.

Midgie read what I had written so far and said it helped her as she had also had an abusive experience. She loves to write, is a natural with computers, and agreed to help me. This book is due in part because of her help and encouragement.

My sister remembered facts I had forgotten, or in some cases just plain didn't know about. She also had a very creative way of putting memories that we had shared.

Anna's expertise as a published author was beyond helpful and much appreciated.

I'm also grateful to 5 Fold Media and Andy and Cathy Sanders for all they taught me, and for giving me this opportunity.

It's my earnest prayer that my story will be a help to others who have been blaming themselves for their abuse—no matter what their reasons are. I believe God wants me to share my story, and He will use it to bring good out of something that was meant for evil.

I may have had a traumatic childhood and awful early marriage, but my life is now enjoyable in both good times and hard. I am thankful for every day. It has been a difficult journey, but I know I am a child of God and have complete assurance I am loved, forgiven, and valuable.

But I Liked It...and Other Lies

Most parents will say, and mean it with all their hearts, that they would die for their children. *I lived for mine.* God graciously spared me from my suicide attempts, but there were literally thousands of urges to die. I now have the skills I need, and suicide is no longer an option in my mind for the first time in my entire life. I'm no longer tempted to harm myself, or have any more suicidal ideations.

DBT has an impressive rate of success, with clients never needing to be hospitalized for depression or self-harming again. I am one of the success stories.

I am deeply grieved for all the hurt and fear my own children have had to live through. I am fiercely sorry they had a mom who was too often unhappy and absent, physically and emotionally. But I *know* that our God can take a crooked thing and make it straight (see Isaiah 45:2).

As Joyce Meyer says, "He's blessed my mess and made it my message." I know He has done this for me, and I trust He will do it for my children.

I no longer yearn for death. Truly, "For me to live is Christ...and to die is gain" (Philippians 1:21). The difference being I want to wait until He chooses.

It is a fact that when the body is touched in certain ways, pleasure is supposed to be felt. This is the way God made us. It is abuse that turns something wonderful into an evil act. I believed my body had betrayed me, because something so wrong brought me pleasure. *What's wrong with me?* I thought.

It's a spiritual, physical, and emotional war. One into which God will go to battle for you. He's rooting for you. The victory is in Him! He died and rose again to set us free, and just as it says in John 8:36—when we are free in Him, we are free indeed.

126

Roxanne Fawley

My daughter, Suzy, used to sing a song based on Isaiah 61:1, ""The Spirit of the Lord God *is* upon Me, because the Lord has anointed Me to preach good tidings to the poor; He has sent Me to heal the brokenhearted, to proclaim liberty to the captives, and the opening of the prison to *those who are* bound... To console those who mourn in Zion, to give them beauty for ashes, the oil of joy for mourning, the garment of praise for the spirit of heaviness" (NKJV). I am now one of the freest, full of beauty, and most joyful of all the people I know!

I have been blessed and changed by the testimony of Joyce Meyer. I highly recommend her books. *Beauty for Ashes*, *Battlefield of the Mind*, and *Power Thoughts* were immensely helpful to me. All of her books that I have been blessed to read have been used by God for me, but these three are my absolute favorites.

Another book I discovered while I was writing mine is *The Wounded Heart* by Dr. Dan Allender. It has a similar message to mine, but from the perspective of a man and a psychologist and with much more research included.

> "Delight yourself also in the Lord, and He will give you the desires and secret petitions of your heart. Commit your way to the Lord, [roll and repose each care of your load on Him]; trust (lean on, rely on, and be confident) also in Him and He will bring it to pass. And He will make your uprightness and right standing with God go forth as the light, and your justice and right as [the shining sun of] the noon day" (Psalms 37:4-6).

This is exactly what God has done for me. When I began to delight in Him, the very desires of my heart began to change and then come true. I've gone from desiring death to loving

127

life, from dreading intimacy with Tom to actually planning for it! From believing and hiding lies to sharing my personal story of God helping me, to His glory, and without any shame on my part! This is the miracle of God's grace. This is what I want for every survivor of any kind of abuse.

> "For I know the thoughts and plans that I have for you, says the Lord, thoughts and plans for welfare and peace and not for evil, to give you hope in the final outcome" (Jeremiah 29:11).

My prayers are with you, my dear reader. Please feel free to contact me. I would love to hear from you and will answer any e-mails personally.

Roxanne Fawley

About the Author

Roxanne Fawley has always lived in Kalamazoo, Michigan. She has a beloved husband of forty years, four grown children, and three grandchildren who all live nearby. She battled depression while being a stay at home mom, but is now a mentally healthy photographer, crafter, and new writer. Thanks to the people who know her and love her anyway, she likes to call herself a professional friend. Her secret to happiness is to start every day loving God and her husband and praying never to believe another lie.

Roxanne can be reached at rocksand5@gmail.com.

Website: www.roxannefawley.com

A portion of the author's profits from the sale of this book will go to the prevention of sex-trafficking, the rescuing of its victims, and the restoring of its survivors.

More Titles by 5 Fold Media

The Valley Without Her
by Amie M. Johnson
$16.95
ISBN: 978-1-936578-71-9

When Emma Leonard disappears without a trace, her family and friends have their world turned upside down. When she is suddenly and inexplicably found, the Thomas family is shaken again, now with a split second decision about what to do. How do they save her? There are so many questions and no time at all for mistakes.

Where has Emma been for nearly two years? What sort of monster would rip a child away from her family? Will anyone ever be the same again? And where is God when His children are in the valley?

Beauty Treatments
by Jodie Dye
$16.95
ISBN: 978-1-936578-63-4

Esther was a young Jewish girl, chosen because of her great beauty to be part of King Xerxes' harem. In preparation for meeting him, she received twelve months of beauty treatments and special food. This book is about a woman who consecrated herself in a similar manner for a different king: King Jesus. As she studied the book of Esther, she discovered many spiritual truths for herself, which are revealed in this book. Applying these *Beauty Treatments* will challenge you, unlocking the inner radiance only available through a closer relationship with the King of Kings for whom our hearts were fashioned.

"To Establish and Reveal"
For more information
visit:
www.5foldmedia.com

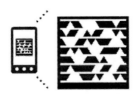

Use your mobile device to scan
the tag and visit our website.
Get the free app:
http://gettag.mobi

Like 5 Fold Media on Facebook, follow us on Twitter

CPSIA information can be obtained at www.ICGtesting.com
Printed in the USA
LVOW12s0006280514

387401LV00001B/1/P

9 781936 578894